Facilitating Posttraumatic Growth

A Clinician's Guide

The LEA Series in Personality and Clinical Psychology
Irving B. Weiner, Editor

Facilitating Posttraumatic Growth

A Clinician's Guide

Lawrence G. Calhoun
Richard G. Tedeschi
University of North Carolina, Charlotte

LEA

LAWRENCE ERLBAUM ASSOCIATES, PUBLISHERS
1999   Mahwah, New Jersey   London

Lawrence Erlbaum Associates, Inc., Publishers
10 Industrial Avenue
Mahwah, New Jersey 07430-2262

Cover design by Kathryn Houghtaling Lacey

Library of Congress Cataloging-in-Publication Data

Calhoun, Lawrence G.
        Facilitating posttraumatic growth : a clinician's guide /
    Lawrence G. Calhoun, Richard G. Tedeschi.
        p. cm.
    Includes bibliographical references and index.
    ISBN 0-8058-2412-X (cloth)
        1. Post-trtaumatic stress disorder—Treatment.   2. Post-
    traumatic stress disorer—Pateints—Rehabilitation.   I. Ted-
    eschi, Richard G. II. Title.
    RC552.P67C35 1999
    616.85'21—dc21   99-18525
                                                              CIP

Books published by Lawrence Erlbaum Associates are printed
on acid-free paper, and their bindings are chosen for strength
and durability

Printed in the United States of America
10 9 8 7 6 5 4 3 2 1

To lifelong friends: John and Carol, Pete and Margaret, Jim and Lisa, Doug and Claudia, Dave and Barb, Arnie and Helene, Nace, Denny, and my best friend, Mary Lynne.
—LGC

઒   ଓ

To Whitten and his family, Chris, Carlton, and Jordan.
—RGT

Contents

Preface

It was with some ambivalence that we began writing this book. Given our identities as "scientist-practitioners," as "scientists" we experienced some degree of hesitation about undertaking a task that required us to build on a small body of empirical research. As "practitioners," however, we felt a need to attempt an articulation of issues of clinical importance on which we have done research for several years, and with which we have had much practical experience. Although it is evident that we overcame our reluctance, it should be made clear that this book represents only our current understanding of the pervasive phenomenon of posttraumatic growth. As research on posttraumatic growth develops, and we hope it will, it may well be that some of our speculations will require modification.

Our goal is to provide a helpful clinical framework for practitioners who provide support and assistance to persons who have faced major calamities in their lives. We seek to enhance their ability to assist these survivors in their quest for meaning, purpose, and growth in the aftermath of their traumas. The range of events that we address is broader than those that are typically identified as precursors to posttraumatic stress disorder (PTSD). The literature on which we have relied includes studies of horrible and repellent events and experiences such as childhood rape, confinement in concentration camps, and life-threatening combat. Our focus is broad enough to include situations that do not involve a direct encounter with a horrible event or a threat to one's own life—situations such as enduring the tragic death of a loved one, surviving the sinking of a ship, becoming disabled as an adult, and facing the loss of employment due to "rightsizing" by a corporation. Such situations confront the average clinician as well as those who specialize in trauma work.

We have written primarily with clinicians in mind. We would be disappointed, however, if researchers found nothing of heuristic value for their investigations of the individual's struggle with the aftermath of highly challenging life events. There are many unanswered questions about the process of posttraumatic growth that only can be resolved by serious and careful research. The reader should consider this book an initial effort to pull together a guide for the practicing clinician , drawing on literature from a variety of different disciplines and a variety of subdisciplines of psychology on the one hand and from our own work as practicing clinical psychologists on the other.

This is not a how-to manual, but we do offer suggestions and examples, as well as construct a framework within which clinicians can make their own decisions about particular persons at particular times. If we achieve the goal we had when we first began to think about the book, then helping professionals and clinical practitioners in a variety of disciplines, including psychology, social work, human services, pastoral counseling, psychiatry, nursing, medicine, family counseling and sociology will find something useful here.

Because this is primarily a clinical book, in the service of utility and reader-friendliness, our citation of references is illustrative rather than exhaustive. Those who prefer a comprehensive citation of works in this area are encouraged to consult the recent collection, *Posttraumatic Growth: Positive Changes in the Aftermath of Crisis,* also published by Lawrence Erlbaum Associates.

We have given specific examples and cited individual cases throughout this book. They are fictitious composites of elements from the experience of different persons at different times, so it is not possible to identify them with any real individuals.

ACKNOWLEDGMENTS

A Reassignment of Duties leave to the first author from the College of Arts and Sciences of UNC Charlotte, Dr. Schley Lyons, dean, was a factor crucial to the completion of this project. We are fortunate to work at an institution and in a department that supports and encourages scholarly activity of this kind.

There are also many individuals we need to thank. Margaret Stanley Hagan, our department chairperson, has provided continuing encouragement and support. Arnie Cann, our friend and colleague, has graciously collaborated with us and lent us his expertise on numerous research projects. Roger Morrell, Jill Gross, Robert Shelton, Wendy Stutts Overcash, Kimberly Hicks, Cathye Jackson, Dottie Fulmer,

Henriette Buur, Jamie McMillan, Paul York, Jacquelyn Loupis, Miriam Torian, and Debora Arnold, our students and our friends, have provided valuable assistance with our work in this area.

Most of all, we wish to acknowledge the clients with whom we have worked over the years. They have demonstrated to us the importance of seeking growth after trauma to feel truly whole. The persons who have faced the ravages of disease, combat veterans, survivors of rape, persons who have become disabled, the bereaved, the unemployed, and others who have seen their lives undone have provided us with examples of the possibilities for change in chaotic times and instruction in how to nurture this change.

Finally, Susan Milmoe, our editor at Lawrence Erlbaum Associates, has been warmly supportive. We appreciate her willingness to give us an opportunity to describe an approach to psychological treatment that goes against the current grain of symptom management, brevity, and directiveness.

—*Lawrence G. Calhoun*
—*Richard G. Tedeschi*

Trauma and Growth:
Processes and Outcomes

Wheresoever you are, death will overtake you, even if you are in lofty towers.

—Middle Eastern Proverb

People tend to operate with certain "positive illusions" (Taylor, 1989) that make the world appear benevolent, safe, predictable, and meaningful (Epstein, 1990; Janoff-Bulman, 1992). However, highly stressful, difficult, and unpredictable events are "neither rare nor unusual" (Freedy & Donkervoet, 1995, p. 7). The lifetime prevalence of major stressful events is high. In a sample of persons from a town in the midwestern United States, 19% reported they had experienced one or more traumatic events in the past year (Breslau, Davis, & Andreski, 1995). In a sample of persons in the southeastern United States, 21% reported a major stressful event such as assault, robbery, or traumatic death of a loved one (Norris, 1992). The frequencies of self-reported traumatic events vary across studies and perhaps across generations (Calhoun, Cann, Tedeschi, & McMillan, 1998; Vrana & Lauterbach, 1994), but exposure to highly stressful events is indeed a common occurrence. If the parameters of what constitutes *traumatic* are broad, then clearly a great percentage of persons, perhaps even all, will experience at least one significant loss, tragedy, or catastrophe in a lifetime.

SEISMIC EVENTS: SHAKING
OR SHATTERING FOUNDATIONS

We use the words *crisis, trauma, traumatic event*, and similar expressions interchangeably as roughly synonymous expressions. It should be clear that other clinicians and scholars tend to prefer a precise distinction between these words, but we do not. Our focus is on events that, to use a metaphor, have a *seismic* impact on the individual's worldview and emotional functioning. Just as an earthquake can produce a dramatic shaking or shattering of physical structures, the events on which we focus in this book produce a severe shaking up, or often shattering, of the individual's understanding of the world (Janoff-Bulman, 1992) and a significant increase in emotional distress (Joseph, Williams, & Yule, 1995).

Some events, such as the Holocaust, are likely to shatter the understanding of the world in all persons who experience them, whereas some events may not even shake the foundations of some people's worldview. From the clinician's perspective, however, the criterion for significant trauma is the degree to which events have been seismic for the individual. This is a transactional view that takes into account the individual's response within the context of a set of environmental circumstances. Traumas occur when a particular type of interaction between a person and challenging events occurs. Our focus is on those life crises, traumatic events, stressors, and tragedies that have an impact strong enough to lead the individual to experience a significant challenge to the ability to order, make sense of, and find meaning in their lives, and which are accompanied by clinically significant levels of emotional distress. The individual's coping ability is severely challenged and he or she may feel emotionally overwhelmed.

Given our somewhat broad and mildly amorphous definition of *trauma*, it is clear that our focus is on a wider range of events than those that are the typical antecedents of posttraumatic stress disorder (PTSD). The sets of circumstances we have in mind include those where individuals are exposed to the life threatening or the grotesque, but they go beyond that strict limitation. The focus of this book is not only on persons who have been held hostage, raped, or who have personally experienced violently destructive combat or other horrible events. We also include the large number of persons who come to the clinician for help in coping with more common, but still emotionally overwhelming, events: the death of an infant from sudden infant death syndrome (SIDS); the loss of one's possessions in a severe storm; a diagnosis of breast cancer; the sudden, unexpected end of a marriage of 30 years because the spouse has left to marry a much younger person; losing one's job at age 56, after 35 years with the same company, because of "downsizing;" the suicidal death of a close family member; and any of the many problems that clients bring to clinicians that represent a severe challenge to their past ways of understanding the world and their place in it, (in other words, events that have rocked and perhaps destroyed the foundations of their way of construing the world).

QUALITIES OF TRAUMATIC EVENTS

What makes events traumatic? In answering this question, a useful perspective is to think of the kinds of events that put individuals at risk for significant psychological difficulties. What are the characteristics of events that lead them to threaten mental health and produce significant psychological distress? In the language that most practitioners employ, what qualities of events make them *traumatic events, major life crises,* or *extremely stressful*? Although no single definition of these terms enjoys universal acceptance, there are several characteristics about which there is significant consensus.

Events that are shocking—that occur suddenly and unexpectedly—are more likely to be traumatic than events that come on gradually and are expected (McCann & Pearlman, 1990; Weaver & Clum, 1995). Circumstances that come on gradually and are expected can also be highly challenging, but the swift, unexpected tragedy or loss tends to be more difficult to resolve. To the extent that individuals can prepare and engage in some anticipatory coping, events tend to be less likely to be psychologically devastating. When an individual experiences the sudden death of a loved one, for example, achieving a sense of resolution and a reduction in long-term psychological pain tends to be more difficult (Weiss & Parkes, 1983).

The most painful and tragic life circumstances tend to be out of the individual's control, and they are seen as such. The perception of lack of control over situations tends to make them more likely to produce subjective distress (Tennen & Affleck, 1990). A key element in events such as armed robbery, rape, loss of house and possessions in a fire, and similar difficulties is that the individual sees circumstances as uncontrollable. Each of these events has clear, direct, painful, and aversive consequences (e.g., bodily injury). An important quality that makes them difficult, even beyond the material or social loss, is in the individual's view that there is nothing that he or she could do about it. In these tragic situations, perceived lack of control is empirically accurate. Many events are inherently irreversible and produce an inevitable sense of powerlessness that can overwhelm even individuals with a strong sense of perceived control over their environments, themselves, and their future. Even in severely threatening circumstances such as armed robbery, the event may be more or less traumatic depending on how much control individuals believe they could and did exercise.

One possible indication that persons believe they have no control over circumstances is by placing blame on others for what has happened. The relationships between blame for the trauma and general psychological adjustment are complex. In general, when the person blames others for his or her misfortune, the psychological consequences are likely to be worse (Tennen & Affleck, 1990). If the individual blames others for the loss, there may be greater difficulty because issues of justice and forgiveness become salient. Such issues may increase the likelihood that the person will become "stuck" in ineffective coping (Falsetti & Resnick, 1995).

Another quality of traumatic events is the threat or experience of physical harm (Green, 1990). Intentional and deliberate harm from another human being (e.g., sexual assault) may be more traumatic and produce more negative psychological response (Tedeschi, 1999), but physical harm from impersonal sources (e.g., tornado, hurricane) can also be a traumatic set of circumstances.

Circumstances that are unusual and out of the ordinary are likely to be more difficult. If events are unusual, they may also be sudden and uncontrollable. Communities and social groups may have some shared knowledge about how to provide support for common events, although they may be highly stressful. People may be less knowledgeable about helping with highly unusual stressors. The death of a loved one is a common loss for which both secular and religious communities have developed rituals designed to provide support and to help with the transition to the new set of circumstances created by death. Communities have no scripts for facing rarer events, such as the disappearance of a loved one: People may not know how to be helpful when a loved one becomes a missing person.

Events that create long-lasting problems are more likely to be highly stressful. Overlapping with the general notion of how long the aftermath of the event persists in daily life is the irreversibility of negative circumstances. Although some events may produce irreversible pain, they are over quickly. For example, if a person is taken hostage during the robbery of a store and she escapes physically unharmed, the event has a clear end and it may not produce any physical change in daily life. If an individual suffers a physical disability that cannot be medically changed, there will be a permanent change imposed on that person's daily routine. The person will now need to face daily challenges of transportation, physical accessibility, social prejudice, and perhaps basic physical self-care. Life stressors that create stressful circumstances that stay with the individual, particularly if the circumstances are not reversible, are more likely to produce significant psychological distress.

The stage of development at which the stressful event occurs may also have an impact on its long-term effects. In general, highly stressful events that occur in childhood are more likely to produce serious long-term consequences for the person. Although sexual assault is a horrible event at any age, it may be more likely to produce long-lasting emotional scars and significant psychiatric impairment when it occurs during the individual's childhood. Most persons are likely to have some general sense of their own identity, of "who I am," by late adolescence or early adulthood. Crises that occur before identity is developed may produce longer lasting scars than those that occur after self-identify provides a means for the individual to integrate the experience into who they are.

Traumatic events are those that are unexpected, perceived as uncontrollable, involve the threat or experience of physical harm, are unusual, have irreversible negative consequences, occur at more vulnerable developmental stages, and involve an assignment of blame to others for one's misfortune. However, we think it helpful to further clarify the kinds of circumstances that are the focus of this book.

THE NEGATIVE AFTERMATH OF TRAUMA

Following is a brief summary of material that is well known to both practicing clinicians and knowledgeable readers of the trauma literature. This section provides a brief summary of some of the common negative responses to trauma. In a sense, to say that life crises have negative consequences is redundant because, by definition, such events cause disruption or distress. This book focuses on the possibilities for growth in the struggle with trauma; it is important to acknowledge that for most people, although not for all (Wortman & Silver, 1989), major life disruptions produce many negative consequences.

Risk of Psychiatric Disorders

When clinicians think about traumatic events, there tends to be a focus on persons who develop posttraumatic syndromes. Lifetime prevalence rates for PTSD have been found by some to be in the 1% to 2% range (Girolamo & MacFarlane, 1996), but some research has suggested the lifetime prevalence rates are actually higher—perhaps around 7% (Kessler, Sonnega, Bromet, Hughes, & Nelson, 1995; Norris, 1992) or even as high as 12% (Resnick, Kilpatrick, Dansky, Saunders, & Best,

1993). As one would expect, rates for PSTD are higher for persons exposed to highly threatening catastrophic events such as military combat. Persons who have been tortured, brutally assaulted, or exposed to extreme combat situations, for example, have much higher rates of PTSD than persons who have lost property but who experienced no physical threat from a natural disaster.

Being exposed to traumatic events also places one at somewhat increased risk for psychiatric disorders other than PTSD (Rubonis & Bickman, 1991). If one examines the personal histories of persons who develop a wide variety of psychiatric difficulties, it is typical for those persons to report higher rates of past stressful events than comparable persons who have not developed psychological troubles.

However, it is important to emphasize that the majority of persons exposed even to the most catastrophic events tend not to develop stress-related disorders (Quarantelli, 1985). Psychopathology is not a necessary consequence of encountering major life crises. Although clinicians are likely to see as clients persons with significant levels of distress and psychological impairment, the practitioner must keep in mind that, in most situations most of the time, individuals may experience significant distress, but they often come through highly challenging circumstances without developing severe psychiatric symptoms. Even in the absence of significant psychiatric impairment, it is common for individuals exposed to highly stressful events to report a common core of negative consequences.

COMMON NEGATIVE CONSEQUENCES
OF TRAUMATIC EVENTS

Distressing Emotions

Emotional distress may be the more salient experience for the individual survivor of a highly negative event. For persons exposed to life-threatening sets of circumstances, a major emotional response is anxiety and fear. For example, a woman who finds the courage to seek shelter from an abusive husband may have physical safety for her and her children as a primary concern (Herman, 1992). In the aftermath of Hurricane Hugo in the Carolinas in 1989, a common emotional response in survivors was high levels of worry and apprehension whenever skies became cloudy and rain was accompanied by even light gusts of wind.

The predominant emotions will vary with circumstance, but along with anxiety, depression is also a common response to stressful events, particularly those involving loss. Sadness is recognized as an almost universal reaction to the death of a loved one. It is typical for persons in grief to be sad, yearn for the deceased, and wish that things could be different (Hodgkinson & Stewart, 1991).

Guilt is another common response to major life crises. It has elements of both thought and emotion, but the guilt that clinicians are most likely to be confronted with in clients is the client's *feeling of guilt*. "Survivor guilt" is a common response among persons who have survived a catastrophe that has not spared others. For example, the father of a child who was severely injured but who was recovering from a school bus accident began to experience a great sense of guilt because he was glad that his child had survived a crash that had killed several other children. He knew he had not committed an unethical act, but he felt bad that he felt so relieved. The experience of guilt may also involve the emotional component connected to thoughts about what the individual might have done or should have left undone prior to a loss. The adolescent daughter of a woman who was hospitalized after a routine appendectomy had a violent argument with her mother about the use of the family car and stormed out of her mother's room and left home for the night. During the night, her mother died suddenly and unexpectedly of a blood clot. The daughter was troubled for a long time after her mother's death, especially about the argument and her sense that she was to blame for her death, because she was not at home to help, and this was because she lost control of her temper.

Anger and irritability are also common responses to life crises. These may not be viewed as having the power that depression and anxiety have to create subjective distress, but these are not pleasant emotions. It is possible that men may be more likely to experience these in the aftermath of trauma than women perhaps because women have been taught better ways to access their emotions of sadness and fear. Regardless of gender, anger is often seen in persons coping with crises. The anger may be expressed directly at those believed to be responsible for the stressful event, like the man who is fired from his job and returns with a gun to settle the score. The anger may be observed simply as an increase in the general level of irritability and increase in loss of temper with targets not even directly connected with the crisis. For example, a woman in hospice care became furious at the apparent "abysmal and repulsive quality of this crap they are making me eat" even when the food was quite satisfactory to others.

Distressing Thoughts

To clinicians, perhaps the most familiar and recognizable component of posttraumatic distress is in the cognitive domain (Horowitz, 1986). For sudden and unexpected events, initial reactions of shock, disbelief, and numbness are typical (Calhoun & Atkeson, 1991; Raphael, 1986). "I just couldn't believe it. I heard the detective, but it just didn't sink in. I was in a fog for the next week" is how the brother of a young man killed in a robbery attempt put it.

The repetitive intrusion of the challenging event into consciousness is also a common posttraumatic response (Greenberg, 1995; Thompson, Chung, & Rosser, 1994). Thinking about it frequently in the early posttraumatic days and weeks, but without wanting to, is almost a signature symptom of posttraumatic stress reactions. A woman in her 20s who had been sexually assaulted by a neighbor when she was 12 said that, "It keeps running through my head like a movie I don't want to see." Even 15 years later she was still haunted by the images of betrayal by a trusted adult. Recurrent thoughts without visual images may be responses that are more common than visual images or troubling dreams.

Intrusive ruminative thought is probably more commonly seen in general clinical practice than intrusive images. This kind of thought process occurs in the wake of trauma when the individual does not want to think about his or her distressing set of circumstances but does anyway. The individual turns over in his or her mind thoughts connected to the difficult life problem. As a man awaiting the results of a biopsy for prostate cancer that physicians had predicted would be positive for cancer said, "I just find myself thinking about it all the damn time. Even if I distract myself with something like TV, something will bring the damn thing back to me, and there I'll be, thinking I better be ready. Am I going to need to wear diapers? Am I going to lose the ability to get it up? Am I going to die?" His remarks made it clear that these thoughts were highly distressing especially because they were out of his control.

We have suggested that traumatic events are those that threaten or destroy the individual's understanding of the world. There have been a variety of attempts to delineate the components of the worldview that are most susceptible to alteration following traumatic events (Epstein, 1990). An important component appears to be the benevolence of the world (i.e., the sense people have that the world is essentially safe for them and their loved ones; Janoff-Bulman, 1992). Persons who have undergone highly stressful events see themselves as more vulnerable to harm than persons who have not (Gluhoski & Wortman, 1996). In addition, persons who have experienced traumatic events tend to see the world as less predictable and less controllable than persons who have not experienced such events (Janoff-Bulman, 1992).

Self-esteem may also be altered in persons who experience traumatic events. Particularly in the time immediately following a trauma, self-esteem may be lowered (Gluhoski & Wortman, 1996). However, in some ways, the individual's self-understanding may change in ways regarded as good, as is seen in the later discussion of posttraumatic growth.

Problematic Behaviors

One way in which behavior can be negatively affected by trauma is an increase in the problematic use of both legal and illegal drugs (McCann & Pearlman, 1990). The judicious use of properly prescribed medication can be helpful to many persons as they attempt to cope with major life crises. The aftermath of trauma can lead to a significant increase in the number of persons using drugs in undesirable ways and in the amount of substances consumed.

The experience of distressing emotions is common, and some persons may assume that others simply cannot understand or help in any significant way (Tedeschi & Calhoun, 1995). Individuals may then withdraw from others, making the use of social support more difficult. If the individual experiences significant depression or if the event involved elements of sexual violence, then another problem may be the emergence of sexual difficulties (Calhoun & Atkeson, 1991).

A final behavioral problem may be an increase in the likelihood of aggressive behavior. A particularly lethal combination is the excessive use of alcohol together with an increase in angry and aggressive behavior. Individuals who are survivors of childhood physical or sexual abuse may be at somewhat higher risk of engaging in similar behavior themselves (Malinovsky-Rummell & Hansen, 1993). This may be particularly likely when the victimized individual's behavior is disinhibited by significant use of alcohol.

Distressing Physical Reactions

Individuals facing the aftermath of major life crises may be at moderately increased risk for physical illness (Herbert & Cohen, 1993). In addition, it is quite common for individuals experiencing major life stress to complain of a wide variety of physical discomforts. The biological mechanisms may involve components of the biological stress response (Selye, 1950). When the crisis is dramatic and sudden, such as a motor vehicle crash or sexual assault, the individual's bodily systems tend to become highly activated; this activation can last for some time after the event is over. Individuals will then report a variety of complaints reflecting prolonged activation of bodily systems: fatigue, muscle tension and aches, difficulty taking deep and cleansing breaths, feeling physically jumpy, and so on.

It is important for the clinician to recognize that a person dealing with the aftermath of trauma can report an array of physical complaints. Some examples are gastrointestinal difficulties, problems with urinary function, a sense of being physically nervous, trouble breathing, a sensation of carrying a weight around, and so on. Under some circumstances, medical referral may be necessary. Perhaps more often, the clinician needs to recognize that this wide array of complaints is a normal response to a highly demanding situation.

Summary

Highly challenging events can produce a variety of negative and unpleasant reactions. Although there do seem to be exceptional persons who do not experience most, or sometimes any, of these negative outcomes (Wortman & Silver, 1989), our experience is that negative reactions to trauma are the clear rule—the exceptions are rare. The pattern of negative response will vary from person to person, but negative elements are likely to be observed in distressing emotions, troubling cognitions, miscellaneous physical complaints, a moderate increase in physical illness, and a small increase in the possibility of significant psychiatric disorder.

This book focuses is on how clinicians can assist clients in the process of growth in the struggle with trauma. We begin with the assumption that persons facing highly negative events will experience negative consequences. It is imperative that the clinician never forgets that suffering is almost always a consequence of trauma.

POSTTRAUMATIC GROWTH

We did not discover the phenomenon of posttraumatic growth. The ideas and writings of the ancient Greeks, Hebrews, and early Christians, and the teachings of Buddhism, Hinduism, and Islam have all addressed the possibility of good coming from suffering. For example, Christianity has traditionally rested on the central role played by the positive consequences of the suffering of Jesus. More recently, other clinicians and social scientists have addressed the possibility of positive change in the struggle with major life crises. Thoughtful social scientists and clinicians such as Frankl (1961), Fromm (1947), Caplan (1964), Dohrenwend (1978), and Yalom (1980) have all addressed in some way the possibilities for positive change offered by critical life problems.

However, it has been only in recent years (O'Leary & Ickovics, 1995; Tedeschi, Park, & Calhoun, 1998) that systematic attempts have begun to be made by psychologists and other researchers to understand, assess, and investigate what we have termed *posttraumatic growth* (Tedeschi & Calhoun, 1995, 1996). Posttraumatic growth is positive change that the individual experiences as a result of the struggle with a traumatic event.

Posttraumatic growth is reported by persons who have experienced all sorts of difficult, tragic, catastrophic, and horrible events. At least some persons experiencing widely different traumatic events (e.g., sexual abuse as children, loss of a home in a fire, the sinking of a cruise ship, the birth of a severely handicapped child, suffering severe injury, the death of a loved one, sexual assault and rape, being diagnosed with breast cancer, bone marrow transplantation, military combat and captivity, and becoming physically disabled as an adult) report being changed in positive ways by their struggle with trauma (Tedeschi & Calhoun, 1995; Park, 1998).

The current research suggests that individuals report posttraumatic growth in three major domains: change in relationships with others, change in the sense of self, and change in philosophy of life.

Changed Sense of Relationship With Others

Crises can impair or destroy relationships. However, a consistent finding in the research on posttraumatic growth is that a significant number of persons report a strengthening of their relationships with others. The positive change is reflected in an experience of increased intimacy and closeness. About 20% of mothers of infants who had serious medical problems requiring the use of intensive neonatal medical care reported that their relationships with family were stronger (Affleck, Tennen, & Gershman, 1985). A woman in her 60s, who had lost her husband to cancer a few months earlier put it this way: "I don't think I have ever been as close to my children as I have in the months since Harold died. I've gotten to know them in a way that somehow just didn't seem possible before. I think I am more real and so are they, if that makes sense."

Both a consequence and a result of the increase in experienced closeness is greater freedom in self-disclosure. Although self-disclosure may elicit undesirable responses sometimes (Dakof & Taylor, 1990), individuals reporting posttraumatic growth in this area regard their increased facility in self-disclosure as positive. In the wake of trauma, individuals can experience an increased need to talk about and discuss their situation, and this need may make self-disclosure easier and more satisfying.

A socially adept executive with a major corporation was diagnosed with a rare and serious form of cancer. His treatment required periodic leaves from work for periods of several weeks, which were in turn followed by stints of several weeks at work. As the cycle continued, with the treatments successful at keeping the dangerous disease from progressing, he found himself focusing more on what he called "the deeper stuff." When colleagues at work asked him how he was doing, he found himself avoiding the superficial and automatic social response, speaking honestly about his current physical state, and articulating more of the "the deeper stuff." As one of his colleagues indicated, there was a reciprocal increase in self-disclosure from others who then began to talk to the man with cancer about their own "the deeper stuff"—particularly their concern and care for him in his battle with cancer.

A widow we interviewed said, "I feel much freer to express my emotions now, because I went through a time when I couldn't hold them back anyway. And now I like it that I can let them just flow with people I trust." The increased sense of freedom in emotional expressiveness is also a manifestation of posttraumatic growth in persons who face major life crises. There can be enhanced freedom in speaking about one's thoughts and feelings, but also in showing them to others. The encounter with suffering can lead people to be more honest, at least with highly trusted others, about what they really think, how they truly feel, and to feel a greater ease in expressing themselves emotionally to others.

Individuals who have "been there too" may experience an increase in empathy and compassion for other persons facing crises. People who have experienced trauma may also be more likely to help others (Wuthnow, 1991). For some persons, there is a marked increase in their experienced sensitivity to the suffering of others. Parents whose children have died, for example, become much more aware of, and feel an increase in compassion for, other parents who have experienced a similar tragic loss. It is not unusual for parents who have lost children to want to somehow be "compassionate friends" to others who are facing bereavement. They report feeling a greater sense of compassion for other parents, engaging in specific small acts of kindness such as sending sympathy cards, and sensing an increased connection to others who are experiencing difficult losses.

Changed Sense of Self: More Vulnerable, Yet Stronger

A consistent finding in the literature on the common negative psychological consequences of trauma is the individual's increased sense that the world is an unsafe place (Janoff-Bulman, 1992) where "bad things *can* happen to people like me." This change in self-perception may be paradoxically both good and bad. On the one hand, it can be bad because the sense of the world as dangerous can produce recurring feelings of fear and anxiety. On the other hand, an increase in one's sense of vulnerability can be a useful corrective to an unrealistic perception that "it can't happen to me."

Such an unrealistic sense of invulnerability tends to be associated with the male gender role in American society and with the adolescent developmental period. Traumatic events can produce an instructional corrective experience. A young man who was permanently injured when his all-terrain vehicle overturned and landed on top of him indicated that he had spent most of his young life taking risks that were foolish. His attempt to ride up a rocky mountain slope, at high speed, without any protective gear was no exception. He sustained a broken neck and several other fractures in the accident. He was not able to walk again. In describing his reactions following the accident, he indicated that he knew full well that he had been "amazingly stupid" in his risk-taking behavior, and that if the accident had not "slowed me down," he would be dead from another accident, in which he might well "have taken out a bunch of other people with me."

This same young man, also described his accident as having taught him just how strong he could be. His view was that if he could handle being in a serious accident, going through months of rehabilitation, and achieving some degree of successful adaptation to the current limitations on his mobility, he could handle just about anything that life could throw at him. The accident taught him that he was vulnerable, but the way in which he coped with the aftermath told him he was strong.

Traumatic events can be highly instructive about self-reliance. This was a consistent theme in what a large percentage of persons who had become widowed told us (Calhoun & Tedeschi, 1989–1990). Coping with the death of a loved one had led them to experience a wide array of challenges, and meeting these challenges had led to an increased sense of the ability to cope with life. The crisis event can set in motion the need to meet a wide array of specific demands, and meeting these successfully can greatly enhance the individual's sense of personal strength.

One of the widows we interviewed—a woman in her early 80s whose husband had died about 15 months before—illustrated how she was changed with the description of a small incident. As she was talking, she pointed out the window to her backyard, which included a well-tended garden. "There used to be a wire fence back there that I really hated. But Lloyd kind of liked it, because he grew peas on it. About 6 months after he died I was sitting right here and looked at the fence and thought: Lloyd wouldn't mind if I took it down now." So, this elderly woman went out to her backyard, by herself, and took down the wire fence. She rolled up the wire and dragged it out to the curb for the trash-collection crew.

Her reaction is reflected in the experiences of many elderly persons, particularly women who have been forced by circumstance to live within the traditional feminine roles. The loss of a spouse may force them to develop expertise in financial matters that had been the husband's responsibility, learn how to deal with service and business people, and decide to seek employment for the first time ever or at least in many years. One woman in her 60s reported that she recently went to driving school and got her driver's license.

There is a substantial research literature suggesting that individuals with moderately high levels of perceived control over events may be better able to cope with life crises (Strickland, 1989). The relationship between perceived control and successful coping is not necessarily simple, but overall having a sense of personal control over life events is psychologically beneficial (Taylor & Brown, 1988). Some individuals who have faced negative events may experience an increase in their sense of competence in meeting the demands of life.

"I know bad stuff can happen to me now, but I think I am much more capable of handling it than I was before" is the theme for many persons. However, the general increase in experienced self-competence is tempered by the sobering reality that "bad things have indeed happened, and they happened to me."

Changed Philosophy of Life

When a person has faced extreme stress (e.g., the death of a loved one or life-threatening illness), he or she must confront the reality of death. That confrontation can lead to a greater appreciation of the value of everyday things. Perhaps one of the most frequently reported manifestations of posttraumatic growth is an increase in one's appreciation of life (Tedeschi & Calhoun, 1995). Persons who have been diagnosed with cancer, for example, may report that they have a more intense appreciation for everyday things: playing with a child, listening to one's favorite kind of music, being more deeply touched by a sunset, or relishing simply spending time with friends.

A related aspect of posttraumatic growth is the experience of shift in life priorities. Most of sinking ship survivors reported that they no longer took life for granted, and three out of four indicated that they now lived each day to the fullest (Joseph, Williams, & Yule, 1993). Changed priorities are reflected in the experience of a highly placed corporate executive who suffered a serious heart attack. He had never been seriously ill before in his life. An almost immediate shift in his priorities after he was released from the hospital was to alter his work schedule so that he would be able to spend more time with his two children, ages 3 and 6. The importance of corporate advancement was no longer the single most important thing in his life—his family was. A typical change in priorities is reflected in these two examples: an increase in the importance of the simple things of everyday life and the recognition of the importance of relationships formerly taken for granted.

Some people recognize as never before that their time, their everyday experiences, and relationships are important. St. Francis of Assissi was asked what he would do if he knew he had only one more day to live. "I would continue to hoe my garden" was his reply. People who have experienced extremely trying circumstances may alter the way in which they view life. Like St. Francis, what they may come to realize is that, if life is indeed short and we as humans are vulnerable to significant losses, perhaps hoeing one's garden may be one of the most important things for us to do.

Herman (1992) suggested that the majority of persons exposed to a traumatic event "experience the bitterness of being forsaken by God." There certainly are circumstances in which the individual's faith is called into question or is destroyed by horrible events. Our own clinical and research experience is somewhat different perhaps because our focus has been on a broader range of events, including many less horrible than those about which Herman has written. In addition, our experience may differ because much of our research has been done in the traditionally religious southeastern United States. We have found that, for many persons, the experience of growth may involve changes in the domain of the spiritual, religious, or existential—changes that can be regarded as a deepening of one's existential experience (Yalom & Lieberman, 1991) and as positive by the individual.

Although persons with traditional religious beliefs may initially experience a loss of faith and a questioning of their beliefs, many report that, in the long, run their beliefs have changed in a positive way (Calhoun, Tedeschi, & Lincourt, 1992). The change can be viewed as positive by some persons who describe their beliefs as stronger and their involvement in organized religion as more frequent. The change can also involve a modification and development of religious beliefs, not necessarily a strengthening of beliefs already held, as the following experience illustrates.

Ashlee F. was a woman in her 30s whose husband was killed during a botched robbery attempt at a fast-food restaurant. He had been taken hostage, but was murdered by the criminal when the police attempted a rescue. In talking about her experience some months later, the woman indicated that the murder of her husband had produced a shaking of the foundations of her faith and that she still had many religious questions about which she was ruminating. She also indicated that since his death she had experienced the sense of being in touch with something transcendent in ways she had never before experienced in her life. Questions had been raised by her loss and remained unanswered, but at the same time her sense of being in touch with spiritual elements of life was clearer and stronger than ever before.

The metaphor of the *thin places* (Gomes, 1996) suggests what happens to some persons as they struggle with traumatic events. In Celtic mythology, the thin places represent locations where it is easier to encounter elements from other dimensions of life—to experience what we might call the *supernatural*. A more traditionally religious view of the thin places regards them as situations in life where individuals have a greater chance of experiencing God or something transcendent; there is a greater chance of encountering the divine other. At least for some persons, periods of crisis lead to a struggle to understand, make sense, find meaning, and cope within the context of a set of religious beliefs and spiritual experiences. The outcome of the struggle is one that the individual regards as positive in fundamental ways.

In Summary

Posttraumatic growth is not uncommon. It has been reported by at least some persons experiencing a wide array of different life crises. The common elements of posttraumatic growth include a changed sense in one's relationships, a changed sense of self, and a changed philosophy of life. Posttraumatic growth can involve an experience of deepening of relationships, increased compassion and sympathy for others, and greater ease at expressing emotions. The change in self-perception may include an increased sense of vulnerability, but an increased experience of oneself as capable and self-reliant. Finally, some individuals report a greater appreciation for life, a changed set of life priorities, and positive changes in religious, spiritual, or existential matters.

But Remember

It is important to keep in mind that not all persons who experience a particular set of circumstances report posttraumatic growth. The available data suggest that between 30% and 90% of persons facing serious crises experience at least some positive change (Tedeschi & Calhoun, 1995). Posttraumatic growth is common, but it is not universal. In addition, there are some sets of circumstances where even the consideration by outsiders that posttraumatic growth may be possible can be regarded by trauma survivors as naive or even obscene. It is not our intent to imply that posttraumatic growth is a facile consequence of a bit of stress. Life crises can have many negative psychological consequences that for some people may last the rest of their lives. What we are suggesting is that, in their struggle with difficult life circumstances, some persons discover that they have changed for the better—that they have grown as individual persons. We hope that we can offer clinicians some useful help as they try to facilitate growth in their clients who face traumatic events.

A FRAMEWORK FOR UNDERSTANDING HOW GROWTH HAPPENS

Before the Trauma

Some persons may be more likely to experience posttraumatic growth than others (Tedeschi & Calhoun, 1995; Tennen & Affleck, 1998). Although the influence of the individual's personality pretrauma may be modest, it is nevertheless potentially influential. Individuals who have a more complex cognitive style, who have higher levels of optimism and hope, who are more extraverted, who are creative thinkers, and who are open to the possibility of new experiences may be somewhat more likely to experience posttraumatic growth (Tedeschi & Calhoun, 1995; Calhoun & Tedeschi, 1998).

The Event and Posttraumatic Cognitive Processing

For posttraumatic growth to be likely, the set of circumstances the individual faces must produce significant psychological upset and a major shaking up of his or her understanding of the world. A worldview includes a general understanding of the nature of the world and the individual's place in it. Philosophers, psychologists, and sociologists have developed a variety of words to describe this general set of ideas (e.g., the assumptive world, higher order schemas), but the compound word *worldview* seems to summarize nicely the idea that people have general sets of ideas and assumptions about what the world is, how it operates, and the individual's beliefs about how he or she fits into the world.

The event that shakes or shatters elements of the worldview sets in motion a significant amount of thinking about the event and its consequences. Some of this cognitive activity is intrusive and automatic. We have chosen the word *rumination* to describe this general process to indicate that the individual spends a lot of energy thinking about what happened. Although the word *rumination* has exclusively negative connotations for some (Nolen-Hoeksema, McBride, & Larson, 1997), we do not use the word in that restrictive, exclusively negative way. The form of cognitive processing of the crisis that we are describing with the verb *ruminate* can include unwanted thoughts and may sometimes involve self-focused negative cognitions. The general process of recurrent thinking that we are describing involves a much broader focus. It includes positive, negative, and neutral cognitive elements, and it can involve more deliberate, thoughtful reflection and pondering about various aspects of the event. As Martin and Tesser (1996) suggested, "rumination is a generic, organizational term that refers to several varieties of recurrent thinking, including making sense, problem solving, reminiscence, and anticipation"(p. 192). This is the general sense in which we use this word throughout this book.

It may be useful to think of the zoological equivalent of the cognitive activity of ruminating. To ruminate, to "chew the cud," refers to the action of some mammals, (e.g., cows), who rechew food to enhance the digestive process. This process involves rechewing in a slow and deliberate way. Most persons who have experienced a traumatic life crisis tend to "chew on it" in the days and weeks following the event. Sometimes this cognitive process is highly intrusive and aversive, as is the case with persons who develop severe symptoms of PTSD. In other instances, the process is less aversive, but somewhat automatic and lacking in premeditated deliberation. The process is characterized by repeated mental revisiting of the event, its antecedents, and its consequences in some attempt to restore some degree of cognitive and emotional balance.

Rumination seems to be necessary to set in motion the process of posttraumatic growth, but intrusive thoughts and images can also be highly distressing. The negative aftermath of traumatic events means that most people need to disengage from a variety of beliefs, goals, and activities. The process of rumination enhances the prospects that disengagement can occur adaptively.

Disengagement is usually a struggle. Part of the adaptive consequence of rumination is that it permits some degree of clarity to emerge about whether a certain goal or activity must be given up. This decision is often unclear; for some persons, it may be a long time before the irreversible permanence of the outcomes are clear and accepted. For example, persons who have sustained permanent spinal cord injuries may believe for some time that they will be able to walk again. Persons who have been diagnosed with terminal cancer may spend all their energies seeking out alternative treatments, hoping for a miraculous reversal of their disease. The difficulty, both for the individual facing the crisis and the clinician who is providing support, is that it is often never absolutely clear what the realistic choice is. As Carver and Scheier (1998) suggested, a major life skill is being able to distinguish between those situations in life where persistence is appropriate and those where disengagement is necessary.

From the clinician's perspective, it is important to remember that, although much of the individual's intrusive rumination is painfully undesirable and unwelcome, chewing on what has happened may well serve a highly useful adaptive function and may well be a necessary beginning to the process of posttraumatic growth. As experts in the process of the development and maintenance of the symptoms of PTSD have pointed out (Greenberg, 1995), and as some research has found (McIntosh, Silver, & Wortman, 1993), the chronic persistence of unabated intrusive rumination is associated with higher and persisting levels of significant psychological distress. It may be that individuals who engage in high amounts of ruminative thought early on, but whose level of intrusive rumination is lower as weeks and months pass, are more likely to experience posttraumatic growth than persons whose level of aversive and intrusive rumination remains essentially unabated over extended periods of time.

It may be that some types of ruminative thought may be more likely to lead to growth than others. To the extent that the ruminations are focused on regrets, current negative emotional states, and negative self-statements (e.g., "I just know I am not coping with this well at all"), one might expect a higher degree of psychological distress (Nolen-Hoeksema et al., 1997). In addition, it may be possible that persons whose ruminative style is highly negative may be less likely to experience posttraumatic growth. To the extent that cognitive processing is focused on remembering positive pretrauma events, on how the individual is going to cope, and on how to make sense or find meaning in what has happened, then one might expect not only less psychiatric distress but also higher levels of growth.

Ruminating about what has happened, about how to sort it out somehow, seems a necessary precursor to posttraumatic growth. However, individuals whose ruminations contain significant amounts of self-derogatory content and who become cognitively stuck may be less likely to experience growth. We have also noted that, at some time after trauma, people may invite an active, deliberate kind of rumination that can usher in significant growth (Calhoun & Tedeschi, 1998).

Emotions: Growth Is Not the Same as Absence of Pain

For most people, highly challenging life events are inevitably accompanied by distressing emotions. Most clinicians appropriately see as their goal the reduction of subjective distress in clients. In thinking about posttraumatic growth, it is important to consider the possibility that some degree of continuing distress about a trauma may be needed for posttraumatic growth to be most likely. Clearly it is necessary for the individual to manage emotions that are strong and sometimes overwhelming. Helping persons reduce distress is a desirable goal. However, it is important to bear in mind that the experience of growth is not the same as the absence of personal distress. Our clinical experience suggests, and other clinicians have noted (Yalom & Lieberman, 1991), that subjective pain and growth may coexist for many persons. This coincides with research that has documented that positive and negative affect are separate dimensions (Bradburn, 1969; McIntosh, Silver, & Wortman, 1993).

The precise relationship between posttraumatic growth and psychological distress is still a matter of investigation (Tedeschi, Park, & Calhoun, 1998). However, it seems desirable for the clinician to adopt a complex perspective in working with clients to enhance the possibilities of posttraumatic growth. Both posttraumatic growth and psychological distress can manifest themselves in a variety of ways. It is not a simple matter of two simple scales, one of which goes up as the other one goes down. It is better to think of a variety of dimensions on which each of these two general domains can vary. There are many possible patterns of relationships between the two general domains of distress and growth. It is also important to keep in mind that not only may growth and distress coexist, but some degree of distress may be necessary for growth to be maintained.

The Influence of Other People

The variety of social groups and communities to which the individual belongs may well have a significant influence on the likelihood of posttraumatic growth. We address this domain more extensively in chapter 5. The individual may learn new ways of thinking about and perceiving the world, may obtain social support, and even may learn new ways of coping from others. The clinician needs to keep in mind that persons who are important to the individual, and who have significant influence over him or her, may provide not only some ideas about posttraumatic growth, but may behave in ways that may enhance or detract from it.

Remember Posttraumatic Growth Is Multifaceted and Client-Developed

The clinician needs to keep in mind what already may be obvious. Posttraumatic growth can occur in some areas, but not others, and it may not occur at all. It may be useful for the clinician to remember the various domains in which posttraumatic growth has been reported as he or she works with clients. A measure we have developed, the Posttraumatic Growth Inventory (Tedeschi & Calhoun, 1996), taps into the five domains of growth to which survivors tend to refer: enhanced relationships, a greater appreciation of life, the opening up of new possibilities for living, spiritual development, and a greater sense of personal strength.

Our view is that it is unlikely that posttraumatic growth can be created by the therapist—it can only be discovered by the client. When the clinician knows that posttraumatic growth can occur in one's changed sense of self, a changed sense of relating to others, or a changed philosophy of life, the clinician will be ready when the client articulates any element of posttraumatic growth.

Story and Identity

Traumatic events may lead to posttraumatic growth by producing fundamental changes in the individual's self-understanding in two broad ways: a change in the general answer to the question "Who am I" and a change in the general answer to the question "What is my life story?" A useful framework for working with clients who face major life crises is to keep in mind these two general questions. Clinicians should try to work with clients in answering these questions. How have clients' identities and how have clients' understandings of their own life narratives been changed? For most persons, their lives are viewed as being bisected by the traumatic event. There is a life before and a life after—who I was then and who I am now, after "it."

Life Wisdom

In some ways, individuals who experience posttraumatic growth appear to show an increase in life wisdom. Individuals who have had to face major challenges in life may be changed by their struggle with difficulties in ways that increase their expertise in the "fundamental pragmatics of life" (Baltes & Smith, 1990). Wisdom can be characterized as the ability to balance reflection and action, weigh the knowns and unknowns of life, be better able to accept some of the paradoxes of life, and to more openly and satisfactorily address the fundamental questions of human existence. Persons who have faced major life crises can come to acknowledge more comfortably the many paradoxes of life. In their loss, there has been gain; the traumatic event is in the past, yet for many it is still very much in the present; the individual's posttraumatic life is changed both for better and for worse; existential questions are more salient, yet answers may be less satisfactory; the individual is more vulnerable, yet stronger. There can be changed priorities, modified philosophies of life, and positive alterations in relationships with specific others and with human community as a whole. Perhaps the same sets of traumatic circumstances that lead individuals to experience psychological growth may also serve as experiences that facilitate the development of life wisdom (Baltes, Staudinger, Maercker, & Smith, 1995).

Summary

A framework that is useful in thinking about the process of posttraumatic growth begins with the occurrence of a seismic event in the individual's life. The crisis severely shakes the foundation of the individual's worldview. There is a significant amount of cognitive turmoil and emotional distress. There is a large amount of ruminative thought devoted to trying to restore some degree of cognitive balance, and there is an increase in coping devoted to reducing the level of emotional distress. Social influences may serve to enhance or impede the process of adaptation and of possible posttraumatic growth. For many clients, posttraumatic growth is incorporated into the individual's identity and life story, with the event serving as a marker event that divides the individual's life into a before and after. The preexisting personality of the individual may have an effect on the likelihood of posttraumatic growth, with persons who are extraverted, hopeful, cognitively complex, and generally open to new experiences being slightly more likely to experience posttraumatic growth than persons who do not have these qualities. Individuals who experience posttraumatic growth may still continue to experience distress related to the traumatic event, and for some persons posttraumatic growth may require that some distress persist to serve as a continuing impetus to posttraumatic growth.

A BRIEF LOOK AT UNRESOLVED ISSUES

Before we undertake the task of discussing how one might enhance the possibility of posttraumatic growth in clinical work, it maybe helpful to provide a brief overview of some unresolved issues in this area. There are clearly many research issues raised by this phenomenon. We do not attempt an analysis of those issues here, because such evaluations are already available (Tedeschi, Park, & Calhoun, 1998). There are a number of important areas on which agreement among researchers does not yet exist or about which the available data are limited or not yet available. It may be useful for clinicians to be aware of two of these areas.

One issue is the degree to which posttraumatic growth involves anything more than the individual's perception of change in the absence of, or at least with minimal change in, observable behavior. There is some small bit of evidence that self-reports of growth may be modestly correlated with reports from other persons (Park, Cohen, & Murch, 1996), and that persons who have experienced crises are more likely to say they have engaged in altruistic behavior (Wuthnow, 1991). However, there is not enough information to say that posttraumatic growth involves clear and observable modifications in how the individual acts. What is clear is that many persons report the experience of growth in the struggle with trauma.

Another unresolved issue of particular relevance to clinical practice is the degree to which posttraumatic growth is associated with overall psychological adjustment. No clear pattern has been observed in the available data (Park, 1998; Tedeschi & Calhoun, 1995). Some studies indicate that posttraumatic growth is associated with overall improvement in psychological adjustment, whereas others show no such relationship. Although it might be assumed that growth would be associated with a reduction in distress, this may not be the case. As others have suggested (Yalom & Lieberman, 1991) and as our clinical experience supports, some significant degree of distress may be required for growth to occur. Perhaps a heuristic point of view is to assume that individual clients can experience positive transformation in the wake of trauma with varying degrees of change in psychological distress or well-being. It is particularly important to remember that growth and distress are not mutually exclusive, and that for some persons growth may only be possible if there is sufficient persistence of psychological pain following trauma. Quick and easy resolutions of crisis may produce no growth at all.

2

Case Examples
of Posttraumatic Growth

This chapter provides clinical cases drawn from our combined clinical experience that illustrate how posttraumatic growth can emerge in clients. It gives an overview of the therapy process and the kinds of interventions therapists can make to encourage growth. The selected cases illustrate the kinds of persons, problems, and discoveries of posttraumatic growth that are likely to be encountered by both clinicians in general practice and those who specialize in trauma work. These are real people, and these are the reports they gave us, with some disguise of personal details.

DIANE: GRIEF AND GUILT

This section begins with the case of a woman who was driving a boat in which her 6-year-old daughter was killed. For 18 months, Diane attended a bereaved parent support group facilitated by one of the authors. This is an edited version of a termination interview done with Diane after she left the group. In it she reflects with one of the group leaders on her experience and the changes she has undergone since the death of her daughter. When she first came to the group, she had been struggling with the degree to which she was to blame for her daughter's death. This had been particularly difficult because she had suffered a head injury and was unable to remember what had happened and because her husband held her responsible. She has since divorced, remarried, and had another daughter. It is now almost 3 years since the accident. We feel that Diane provides a good description of the mixture of growth with the continuing pain.

Therapist: Looking back, how are you different now?

Diane: Probably I'm more cautious than I used to be, especially with Caroline. Things I would let Alice [her deceased daughter] do, I don't let Caroline [her other daughter] do. Things like leaving her in the bathtub without being right there on top of her. Caroline wears a helmet on her tricycle. Most people don't think about that, and I do. I guess I'm just more cautious, bordering on paranoia.

Therapist: You find yourself thinking about things that could happen a lot?

Diane: Not things that could happen to me, more my daughter. The effect of Alice's death has been transferred from me to Caroline. As far as how I do things or treat myself, it hasn't affected me as much as it has how I deal with Caroline.

Therapist: What about the way you deal with other important people in your life?

Diane: I'm a lot closer to my family now than I used to be. I make more of an effort to visit and do things with them, and I also rely on them more. It is clearer to me that they are there.

Therapist: So you accept their help more than you used to.

Diane: Yes, and the same with friends, and that sort of thing. I'm not afraid to show them I'm upset. I don't care who knows it. If I'm sad, I'm sad, I don't care who knows it. If I'm happy, I don't care who knows it. I'm more free with my expressions and I'm not particular about a setting. I don't get embarrassed easily, I guess like I might have been before.

Therapist: You're freer, more expressive.

Diane: Right. And I value friendship more than I used to. The more friends you have, the more support you have when you need it, but you're able to support them if they need it. And I'm more curious about things. I ask a lot of questions and I look at things. You know if someone is talking about any aspect of death, I'm more interested in that. I'm interested in other people's experiences.

Therapist: You focus on different things now.

Diane: I think I also try a little harder to attain a goal. I've gone back to school, and I'm more determined to get a degree. Before I was just floating along. Now I want it. I want to establish myself and be more self-reliant.

Therapist: So even though you were in school before …

Diane: The drive wasn't there to do it. I'm more motivated now. Sometimes I look at it and say it's because Alice knows what I'm doing, and because she's not here, I have to do it.

Therapist: You want to do it partly for her as well as yourself.

Diane: Right. And yet I'm cautious. It's unbelievable, I try not to be like that, but I can't help it. My neighbors laugh at me because I've had the fire department out probably twelve times in three years.

Therapist: How so?

Diane: Only one gas leak and a fire. The other times I've been afraid of Caroline being injured. She fell down the stairs, she fell off the bed—stuff like that. Part of it might be my experience with the [bereaved parents] group. I didn't think of all the ways kids could die. Now whenever something happens similar to what I've heard … like I went and had some heart tests done on Caroline—that's super-paranoid. But there's no way I can see myself settling down with that. I can't help the way I am now, or don't want to, or don't know how to.

Therapist: Is there anything positive to this caution?

Diane: It's good in some ways. Some of it has rubbed off on Caroline. She'll think before doing something crazy. She won't walk into something she's not familiar with, she'll check first. She just won't go into the street, because she's afraid of getting hit. I guess that's the positive part. But I don't want her to become a chicken, either.

Therapist: I've been thinking back to how hard it was for you to come to grips with the way the accident happened and whether you were responsible. It seems that you have come to terms with that to a great extent.

Diane: That has been so hard, because I will never really know what happened. Maybe it is a blessing that I suffered that head injury. But I have come to realize that my intentions had always been to protect her, that I can be sure of. And the discussions in the group that showed me that everyone felt like they let their kids down somehow—that helped me. No matter what happened, as a mom, I would feel that I didn't do my job of protecting because my child died.

Therapist: It seems like it was scary for you to consider these questions for a while.

Diane: Yes, but I think the group finally got to me. I guess I had to learn that they supported me no matter what. So I remember talking about the accident, and how that other boat cut in front of me. And how I was sure that Alice had her life jacket on, but that she drowned without it. It did take me a long time to get that out. But it was always in my mind. I had to deal with it to get through my grief. But there will always be a question about it for me. I've faced it, but I guess it will always remain a question, too. I guess the difference is now I can live with it.

Therapist: The group played a big role in this part.

Diane: Oh yes. I don't know what I would be like if it weren't for the group. It's probably a lot of the reason for a lot of the changes I've had—being stronger, knowing it's okay to express your feelings, and knowing your not the only one, knowing that there are other people who know exactly what you're dealing with. I'm more compassionate toward other people. Because I can understand it all. I think the actual loss, the feelings and all that, is the same, no matter who your child was, how old they were. Dealing with other people, that's the hard part. Now, I'm like, I don't care what you think.

Therapist: The people that haven't lost children.

Diane: Right. Which, it's understandable, but what do you do with that? It's part of protecting yourself, too, and part of feeling sorry for yourself. This happened to me, and I don't care what you think. It sounds mean, and I guess it could be taken that way. But part of it too is you're trying to deal with it and it's better to express it than hold it in, if that makes sense.

Therapist: It's a combination of not caring what they think …

Diane: Yes, but it's not intentional to hurt somebody else, to make them feel bad. It's to make yourself feel better.

Therapist: It's expressing yourself if that's what you need to do without being concerned about the effect it has on people that haven't lost a child.

Diane: Right. That gets better with time. I'm a little more conscious of jumping right in. Some people just fall over backwards when you say that, they just don't know what to do. I don't do that like I used to.

Therapist: You're more sensitive to the effect it has.

Diane: A little bit more than I was. But at the same time I really don't care. This is me and I'm the only one in my situation.

Therapist: Before you were more concerned about expressing your own feelings because that was what you needed. But now you've gotten to the point where you can monitor the effect that it's having but yet you can also express yourself.

Diane: Right.

Therapist: You try to integrate these together. I think that would be really tough.

Diane: Yes, that's one of the hard things. But everybody else that's done it, has experienced it, has done the same thing.

Therapist: So it helps to talk with other people.

Diane: Oh yes. The biggest thing was knowing that you could survive it, that you are going to be okay. That there is a light at the end of the tunnel, even if you can't see it. But you don't really know what you are doing either.

Therapist: Everybody has to figure out their way of dealing with it.

Diane: Well, you don't figure it out, you just sort of do it. You can't decide anything. Each day you just go along and do what you need to do that particular day. There's no plan.

Therapist: But I get the impression that has changed for you at this point.

Diane: Well, number one, dealing with that and dealing with other problems in life are two totally different things. I think you become stronger, and I think that no problem is too hard, no problem is too difficult, no problem is going to put you under. Everything can be dealt with.

Therapist: Not only do you feel you can handle problems, you can.

Diane: Yes, nothing is as bad as that. That's the worst that can happen. And believe me I've dealt with a lot. That was the worst. It makes you stronger emotionally. You just keep plugging along because you feel like what else can happen that's going to be that bad?

Therapist: But when Caroline got sick [she developed a rare bacterial infection], it *was* like something that bad.

Diane: When they told me she had only a 10% chance, I thought, my God, if I lose another one, that's it. But I had everybody there, people just showed up, and I knew that's what I had to do. I knew I couldn't do it by myself. And that worked. My sister asked me after Caroline had made it, if she hadn't made it what would you have done? She asked me if I had thoughts of killing myself. I said yes. That's something I don't think I could ever handle again. But there again, until it's happened, you don't know.

Therapist: You weren't sure what you'd do.

Diane: You face it and either you make it through or you don't. But the more support you have, the better your chances of dealing with something that's too tough to handle. So that's something that I learned.

Therapist: For you, that support hasn't seemed to include religion.

Diane: I don't have any desire to build on my faith or lack of it, or understand any of it. I've gone to church a couple of times since she died and it doesn't do a thing for me. More so than before, I don't know what to believe. I have a real block when it comes to religion right now. The idea of the church helping and being supportive of the community and doing good deeds and people getting together and doing good for whoever, God or anybody else, is a good thing. As far as there being someone to worship who takes care of everybody, who puts us here and protects us, I question that. People can say there was a reason, but it wasn't a very good reason. Tell me what it was. That doesn't fly with me. I'm very skeptical when it comes to that kind of thing now. Whereas maybe 20 years ago I wasn't.

Therapist: Along those lines, how would you say your life philosophy or goals have been affected?

Diane: I want to do more and see more. Get involved with things, and I want Caroline involved, too. There's a whole world out there to see and I haven't seen a lot if it.

Therapist: In terms of travel?

Diane: Anything. I tend to pay more attention to the news and read books more than I used to. I like to read articles and magazines. I like to listen to people and speakers on different subjects. I go to seminars for no reason but that I'm interested. I just want to find out about more things. I want Caroline to do the same—be curious about things. Like I'm intellectually more curious in a lot of ways. That could be due to age. It might not have anything to do with what happened. Except the way I deal with Caroline. Most of how I've changed is centered around her. Alice's death affects that tremendously.

Therapist: Like being more cautious, but at the same time encouraging curiosity.

Diane: Yes, and being open about things. Like Alice. I think about her and talk about her, and sometimes Caroline asks questions about her. Sometimes I'm afraid I might push it too much, because she'll say that she doesn't want to go upstairs because she might get sick and die like Alice. I might have gone overboard with her pictures and movies, but that's my way of remembering her, through Caroline.

Therapist: This keeps Alice as part of your family.

Diane: She'll always be a part. But now I can let go of things from the past better. I've given away some of her things, which I never thought I'd do. They just take up space, I don't need them anymore. So I'm getting a lot stronger in realizing that life goes on. It doesn't mean I have to forget Alice. But it means that you have to continue with your life and you can remember in your own way. You can have pictures, some things. You can't hold onto the past forever.

Therapist: It was an important step for you to give away some of Alice's things, but some you keep.

Diane: There are some clothes I won't give away to my niece. But I'll let Caroline play with Alice's old things. They won't get lost, but they might get broken. It's a whole process, and I think your whole life you're dealing with it, and your whole life, something's going to come up that has to do with it, and you're always going to be affected by it. I don't think there's ever going to be a day until the day you die that you don't deal with it.

Therapist: It's always there, always in the back of your mind, although maybe in a different form now.

Diane: And it affects you in so many different ways, good and bad. And you're dealing with it every day. Whether you know it or not, you are.

In this interview, it is clear that Diane can see both the continuing grief as well as the growth that she has experienced as a result of her daughter's death. To us, this makes the descriptions of posttraumatic growth credible. The vast majority of people who mention it do not deny the pain they have suffered and state that they continue to suffer.

Because this was a session conducted after Diane had completed attendance in a support group, the therapist is simply reviewing and closing up this group experience, rather than conducting an individual therapy session. So we do not see in this example specific interventions by the therapist. The following examples are from therapy sessions where growth-facilitating interventions are more evident. For each case, we provide a narrative introduction, a summary of some individual sessions with some illustrative exchanges between client and therapist, and a case discussion.

LUCIA: PAST AND PRESENT CRISES

Lucia was born in Peru, but her parents moved to the United States when she was still an infant. Her early years were spent in a multiethnic neighborhood in Florida, in which persons of South American origin predominated. She grew up bilingual and, in a sense, bicultural. There was clearly the influence of American culture, but her family also maintained the views, values, and assumptions of her South American heritage.

By the time Lucia was 8, she had two younger siblings, ages 6 and 2. Her recollection is that she was occasionally verbally abused by her mother from very early on. The abuse occurred rarely, but it involved being called *stupid, ugly, idiot,* and similar things. Her mother did use corporal punishment, but Lucia does not consider it to have reached the level of physical abuse. It did with her father. She remembers him as a "very angry man" who would routinely hit her. Many times she was not sure why he had hit her, but the physical abuse was usually accompanied by verbal abuse, similar to her mother: *little whore, stupid,* and *ugly* are some of those Lucia recalls.

In the third grade, she was sexually molested by an 18-year-old neighbor. Her recollection is that she was "seduced rather than forced." She describes him as a smooth talker and as being "what seemed to me at the time as kind." The abuse lasted for only a few weeks and ended when her mother accidentally interrupted an incident. She told Lucia's father, who in turn sought the young man out and told him that he would "be dead by morning." Lucia's recollection is that the young man left to live with relatives in another city and she never saw him again.

At the age of 14, she was drugged and raped at a party. She told no one except her mother, who called her a *whore* and threatened to tell Lucia's father but never did. She never spoke about the rape again until she entered treatment.

When Lucia was 16 and a junior in high school, her father, who had moved out of the house some months before, stabbed the man her mother had been seeing and threatened to kill her mother. Although serious, the stab wound was not life threatening, but both her mother and her partner were terrified that Lucia's father would follow through on his threat. They made a quick decision to move. They left Florida and moved to a large city in the northeast.

The move was traumatic and difficult for Lucia. She was now in a strange city, she was no longer in a cultural community in which she felt comfortable, and she quickly developed noticeable symptoms of clinical depression. She felt lonely, unhappy, and very sad; she felt she had no friends at all and simply wanted out. She attempted suicide one evening by swallowing 25 over-the-counter pain pills and was admitted to a local psychiatric facility. She stayed 3 days and was released. She was seen by a psychologist for follow-up and outpatient treatment.

Early Sessions

The focus of the first session was on Lucia's current and past functioning. She was still quite depressed, but no longer actively suicidal. The session was a rather typical "intake" with a bright young woman who had been experiencing significant clinical depression. The clinician's judgment was that outpatient treatment was appropriate and continuation of antidepressant medication was important. The clinician was successful in beginning a good therapeutic alliance, and Lucia agreed to subsequent visits with him.

In subsequent sessions, more of Lucia's history and background emerged. She talked about her bicultural background and implied, but did not directly articulate, that her parents, her father in particular, had been abusive. The clinician's decision was to not yet confront or probe about the past abuse, because there was no indication of abuse in Lucia's current situation. In discussing her background, she mentioned that she had grown up as a "South American Catholic in a North American neighborhood." The clinician decided to probe further.

Therapist: I am not sure that I actually know what it means to be a South American Catholic in North America. Can you help me understand that better?

Lucia: Well, for me it was kind of a mixture. I guess when I say Catholic, I mean we did all of the traditional things, like first communion, we went to church on the important days like New Year's Eve, and every few months my parents would take me to confession. I thought of myself as Catholic, at least in the sense that I gave myself the same label that my family did. The church we attended was bilingual, and most of the things I was involved in were in Spanish. It was more like being a Republican or Democrat in politics. It's just sort of the group that you say you belong to. It was not, for me, a real spiritual or religious thing particularly. It influenced my thinking some, but not a lot.

Therapist: How would you describe yourself now?

Lucia: I am not sure. I still call myself a Catholic, and I still have a belief in God. With what I am going through right now and what happened to me before, it has me a little confused about lots of things, this kind of stuff too.

Therapist: So you still have some kind of belief in something beyond you, but your life circumstances have kind of stirred your beliefs up some.

Lucia: Yeah, I guess you could pretty much say that.

The clinician probed a bit further about her current spiritual feelings and views and how these related to her more recent difficult life experiences. Toward the close of the session, the clinician asked about her current prescription for antidepressants and made a brief evaluation of her current depressive symptoms. There were still clear signs of clinical depression, and Lucia indicated she planned to continue to take her medicine as prescribed.

In the seventh session, Lucia gave her first clear indication that she had experienced some major stressors in her life, slowly revealing that she had been sexually molested in the third grade and that she had been raped when she was 14. As the therapist led her through a description, at her own pace, of what had happened, Lucia repeated two or three times that she could not believe that she had not been "totally wiped out" by what had happened to her. Her discussion suggested the possibility of an implicit perception of strength. The third time Lucia talked about this, the therapist decided to tentatively look at that possibility.

Session 7

Therapist: So you look at the horrible things that have happened to you in your life, and you think that given how horrible those things were it is pretty remarkable that you are doing as well as you are.

Lucia: Yeah, I guess you could say that. Sometimes I just can't believe I am not a complete whacko, you know?

Therapist: When you say that, you know the kind of image that comes to my mind? It's like you are a professional boxer, I mean in the ring with this heavyweight champion you are fighting. And he has punched you really hard two or three times. Both he and the crowd expected you to be knocked out cold on the canvas. But look here you are, not only are you not knocked down, but you are still standing and punching back!

Lucia: Well, it's not like he didn't touch me, because after all, I did take those pills, you know? So I have felt lots of pain from getting hit, like you say, but I guess so, I'm not out yet.

Therapist: Just being able to stay on your feet is a pretty big accomplishment.

Lucia: I guess you could say so. Maybe the fact that I am not a complete whacko means that I can take a few of those professional boxer punches and survive.

Therapist: Sort of like that saying about just surviving is a sign of strength.

Lucia: Could be I guess. Maybe that is kind of like me.

By the ninth session, which took place about 14 weeks after the first, Lucia's active depressive symptoms were considerably reduced. She was still experiencing occasional feelings of sadness and her self-esteem was still somewhat low, but things were noticeably better for her. She had made some attempts to make friends and had, in her words, "two new friends now." She was still anxious about her relationships with guys—a concern that her clinician estimated would be an issue for Lucia for some time. These concerns were clearly connected to her history of molestation, abuse, and sexual violence. Problems still remained, but there was not only clinical improvement of the psychiatric symptomatology, but also some manifestations of posttraumatic growth. In Session 7, she had begun to talk about herself as stronger than she previously had thought, and this theme continued through subsequent weeks. In Session 9, she articulated a change in her view of interpersonal relationships especially with men.

Session 9

Lucia: I guess things are better than they were when I first did the pill thing. I think my medication has helped some, and I think talking to you has helped some too.

Therapist: How would you say things are better now?

Lucia: Well, I have a couple of girlfriends, and I don't feel as lonely as I did. My mom and her boyfriend are planning to get married, and being away from my dad and his crap has been great. We have not heard from him, and right now, I hope we never do.

Therapist: So, things are better at home, you have some friends, and the worry about your dad has gone. How about with guys, how is that going?

Lucia: Well, you know, I am not sure. I think about that a lot. I mean, I want to have a boyfriend and all that. But I know that I have to watch out and be careful about what kind of guy I start to hang out with, you know.

Therapist: How do you mean watch out and be careful?

Lucia: It's like, well … I don't want a guy who is going to treat me like my dad treated my mom. I obviously do not want a guy who is going to force himself on me or even try to control me, you know. I know how bad some guys can be, and I do *not* want anyone like that. So I guess what I am saying is that, like you said one time, there is a lot worse stuff than just being alone, you know.

Therapist: So, in a way, having to deal with what happened to you, having to struggle with that, seeing what you saw, experiencing what you did, and having to survive all that … makes you want to make sure that you take some care when you develop relationships with guys.

Lucia: You bet, but I know this is not going to be easy.

For Lucia, there was no single, clearly specifiable traumatic event. She underwent two major traumas (molestation and rape) and also had a long history of childhood abuse. The event that precipitated treatment was her suicide attempt following her move from one end of the country to the other.

The first sessions were devoted to gathering information and building a relationship with Lucia. There was no hint of even the possibility of posttraumatic growth for several weeks. At that point, the therapist saw an implicit theme of perceived increase in self-perceived strength and made the decision to label it as such, but in such a way that Lucia could disagree. It was, in this case, a right decision. She had been considering the possibility that maybe she had proof of her strength simply because she had some horrible experiences, and yet she was not "whacko." As opportunities arose in subsequent sessions, the clinician would seek intermittent opportunities to reinforce Lucia's description of her perceived strength.

The metaphor of the boxer taking and withstanding the heavy blows of a strong opponent proved useful and successful here. Lucia was to mention that particular image again in subsequent sessions. Not all attempts at metaphors work this well or this easily. The therapist may need to experiment with alternatives, focusing on images and metaphors that are useful therapeutically.

The other manifestation of possible posttraumatic growth did not appear clearly until a later session. It reflected a theme that has been reported in the clinical literature (Veronen & Kilpatrick, 1983). Lucia's exposure to and struggle with abuse and sexual coercion had led her to want to make good choices about relationships with men. She wanted to have some good anchors about what good and negative relationships between men and women should be, and she wanted to make a conscious effort to choose good relationships with good people.

Lucia experienced chronic abuse and at least two instances of heterosexual betrayal and violence. Lucia entered long-term psychotherapy and her sessions are still ongoing. The specific themes of posttraumatic growth have become an integral part of Lucia's understanding of who she is—what her "life story" is. Treatment, of course, was broader and more far ranging than the specific focus on posttraumatic growth. The clinician recommended a medical consultation for antidepressant medication, there were uses of cognitive techniques in several sessions, there were homework assignments of various kinds, particularly cognitive work in the earlier sessions, and there was also some role-play about social situations and issues. In summary, treatment was eclectic, but the clinician was alert to opportunities to notice, label, and reinforce posttraumatic growth perceived and discovered by the client.

HUGH: MAKING A MESS OF THINGS

Sometimes the trauma that sets growth into motion seems to be created by a person who needs to change, but has to disrupt current life to get to the growth. The following is an example of a 51-year-old man who seems successful in every way. He is bright, financially sound, happily married, very active in his church, a top executive for a big telecommunications company, and has a daughter who is winning awards in high school for athletics. He came to therapy after having had a sexual liaison with a prostitute while on a business trip. In the process, he found his credit card missing and suspects the woman took it. He stated he had never done anything like this before. He confessed to his wife when he returned home, and she told him to leave. She said she would only consider taking him back if he could find out why he did this. Hence, psychotherapy.

In the first couple of sessions, Hugh and the therapist review in detail the events surrounding his decision to find the prostitute, to discern his motives. It emerges that, despite his apparently perfect life, Hugh was undergoing stresses and suppressing nagging questions about how he was living.

Hugh: I had accepted an invitation to go on a speaking tour of Europe for my professional organization. This was a major coup. But you know, I was aware of how this was really going to stress me, and that the company wouldn't really give this any consideration in their expectation for how I was going to handle some of our projects in the next few months. And you know what? The night I came home after accepting this great invitation, my daughter tells me that I'm never around enough to have any idea about what she's doing. I've felt for a long time that nobody appreciates how hard I work for them—the company or the family. I'm on this treadmill running like hell.

Therapist: You haven't talked to anyone about this?

Hugh: I'm afraid if I said anything to Nancy [his wife] she'd get upset because she'd think I was planning on making less money—then what would happen to her nice lifestyle? And you don't say things about this at work—they'd begin to think you can't cut it anymore. And a guy my age has to be careful not to encourage those perceptions.

Therapist: So you've been alone with these thoughts and feelings.

Hugh: Well, I haven't even paid much attention to them myself. I've just tried to push on.

Therapist: But these concerns started to become more insistent?

Hugh: That night I just got to the point I needed someone to talk with. I was thinking that a girl might be real sympathetic, just listen to me. Isn't that stupid? But I thought I could just call a girl, and she'd be sweet and listen to me.

Therapist: You weren't thinking of sex with her?

Hugh: I really don't think so. That's just not me. You may find that hard to believe, but I really believe that. When she got undressed, I was kind of shocked. When she said she wanted me I just started to go along with it. Then I sort of came to and went into the bathroom. I told her to leave, and I think that's when she took my card. Then it all really became a nightmare. I literally sweated through the night. I was thinking, "this just isn't me!" I knew I'd have to tell Nancy. I started thinking I might have AIDS. I wondered how I could go back to church, how I could look people in the eye. I couldn't believe what a mess I made of things and hadn't really meant to.

Therapist: Of course, this really was you doing all these things.

Hugh: But it didn't seem like any me I knew anything about.

Therapist: I guess you began a process of learning about yourself, and we're continuing it right here.

Hugh: I'm not too pleased with what I'm finding out.

Hugh paid a visit to the health department to get checked for sexually transmitted diseases. He decided to go there because he didn't want his family doctor to know what he had done. At the health department, Hugh met a woman who has AIDS. This woman was kind and supportive to him in his anxiety. This encounter made him think about his way of relating to others, and his priorities.

Session 3

Hugh: So here I am in the health department, this upper middle class white guy, and this young woman with AIDS is comforting me. What's wrong with this picture?

Therapist: Not a circumstance you ever imagined you'd be in.

Hugh: Never in a million years. But it made me think about the circles I travel in. I've always thought that I see a lot of the world, but there is a lot I never see. People like her. You know, when I was in college back in the 1960s, I was an idealist. I was going to do something to change things. I sure have—I've made a lot of money. I'm not sure I'm satisfied with that anymore.

Hugh went back to the health department for initial test results after this session and returned with the following report at the next session.

Hugh: Well, I don't have any STDs. I'll have to get rechecked for AIDS again in 6 months and 1 year. In the meantime, Nancy and I don't have sex. I wonder what that will mean for us.

Therapist: I thought you were separated.

Hugh: Yeah, but we've been talking quite a bit, and she's glad I'm in therapy and dealing with this. I can tell she still loves me. I'm hopeful we'll get through this. I feel bad I've done this to her, and I really want to make things right. I'll do whatever it takes.

Therapist: This is different for you?

Hugh: I've always been a guy who would do whatever it takes, but maybe I was focused on the wrong things. Not the wrong things, but I'm not sure my priorities have been straight. You know, I've always told myself I was working so hard for my family, but it was really for myself, for recognition. I think I've been fooling myself about that. In the end, what does recognition matter? We're all the same, all the same fragile people. Like that woman at the health department. She didn't know I was some accomplished guy with money. I was just a nervous, ashamed, worried guy waiting for his test. You know what? When I went back for the results, she was there, and I told her how much her kind words meant, and she hugged me. I told her I was going to do something about AIDS. Do you believe it? This is getting strange, I don't know what I was talking about, but it just seemed right.

Therapist: It sounds like you've taken the blinders off.

Hugh: When I say I'm going to do something, I do it. I don't know what it is yet, but I'm not going to forget. Being in that health department, it just struck me that I always thought about people with AIDS as low life or deserving it. But you know, people make mistakes. I made a mistake, and I could be one of "them." This woman with AIDS, I think she's a better person than me. She's got more problems than me, yet she was the one reaching out. I don't know whatever happened to Hugh the idealist.

Therapist: It sounds like he found his voice—spoke up about doing something about AIDS.

Hugh: Maybe so.

The therapist simply notices the positive developments. It is not necessary to make any grand statements about them. Some are not even labeled at this point—for example, the improving relationship Hugh is developing with his wife or his changing priorities. It is still early in the therapy and in the process of change, and further advances seemed likely to appear. The therapist has to discern when the time is right to highlight posttraumatic growth. When it is still early, it can seem like overplaying the changes to suggest that they are of great import.

Session 6

Hugh: I've decided to make at change a work.

Therapist: What's that?

Hugh: We've been talking for a while about implementing a recruitment and mentoring program for women and minorities, and I've talked with (the CEO) about heading it up. He was surprised, but I was clear I wanted to do it. So I'm switching out of my area to do this. It is a foolish career move, but further advancement isn't really of interest to me anyway. And I turned down that Europe trip. Called them up and told them I was too busy. Can't believe it.

Therapist: So how does all this feel?

Hugh: Great! I think I'm seeing things more clearly, what's important, what's really me. I feel lighter and energized. It's the strangest thing. You know what else? I've got a big presentation tomorrow that I'd usually be very anxious about, wanting to impress and wondering what people think. But I've hardly prepared. I've been thinking, "I know this stuff already, and if they don't like my ideas, too bad. I'll put them out there and we'll see what happens." And I wrote a letter to the CEO telling him what I thought about his plan for the acquisition, not critical or anything, but I never would have voiced my opinion like that before. You know, even if I lose my job, I know I could get one pretty quickly—I've got a good reputation, and I do good work.

Therapist: You're not worried anymore about what people think, or what will happen.

Hugh: It's funny, these are the best of times and the worst of times. I've done something terrible to put my marriage, my life, in jeopardy, yet I feel better, liberated. A strength to be myself.

Therapist: You've got a new perspective on what's worth worrying about.

Hugh: I seem to. But I wonder if I'll go back to my old ways.

Therapist: This might wear off.

Hugh: But you know, I feel enlightened, and I don't think I could ever go back. I might slip a little, but I don't think I'd go all the way back. And doing things differently just feels so much better.

Here the changed perspectives and new priorities are put into action. Perhaps to the person who knows Hugh only casually, these changes don't seem that large. He's still working for the same company, still a big executive. But to Hugh, his focus has shifted dramatically.

Session 8

Therapist: How do you understand now what has happened to you?

Hugh: I still don't really understand it. I think I was on the wrong track and something had to give. I don't think I was paying close enough attention to how I was living, and maybe I needed to have something pretty dramatic to get my attention. I hate that I did what I did, but I've prayed for forgiveness and have told God that he'll see my sincerity in how I change. I think this goes for Nancy, too. She needs to know I won't betray her. If I just live the same way, whose to say I won't go wrong again? But mostly, I just feel I need to do some things differently to be true to myself.

Notice that Hugh is now viewing his wife as a partner to be reassured, rather than his earlier view of her as expecting a lifestyle he needed to support through demanding work. Also notice that although Hugh still hates what he did, he has transformed his sin into redemption. So his act and the suffering it caused are not in vain, and he can live with this and himself.

By the 12th session, Hugh had begun to push the envelope on life changes even more. Feeling more confident and recognizing his value, he sought out new career opportunities.

Session 12

Hugh: I've been talking with those headhunters and suddenly I'm getting lots of attention from around the country. I had an interview last week with [a competitor with his current company] and another with the [federal regulators in his industry]. And I contacted someone in the main office in New York about what I could do to help now that this acquisition has happened. They are very interested, and I'm going to talk with them next week. And you know what? After feeling undervalued for years in my position, I'm looking at huge salary increases in these things. But at the same time that I'm clearer on my value, I'm perfectly willing to turn anything down if it doesn't work for me personally and for my family. I'm telling these folks right off that I have my limits on travel and work hours. I'm up front from the start. I'm getting amazed at myself.

Therapist: Still learning about this new Hugh.

Hugh: I feel like the invincible, vulnerable man. I've found out how badly I can get myself off track. How I really need to pay attention to what's going on with me. And I guess I've gotten a little angry about how I've been doing things, and I'm determined to change them. I feel like nothing can hurt me now. Even if I lose my job, I see I can find another. I don't have to cling to this position, always trying to prove my worth.

Therapist: But there are worse things than losing your job.

Hugh: Sure. I've thought of that. What if I find out that I do have AIDS? Well, I won't like it, but I'm convinced I call deal with it. I'd feel guilty because I brought it on myself, and Nancy would have a right to be even more angry with me. But I see no sense in getting really miserable about it. I've got to get a biopsy for this growth on my colon. What if I have cancer? I'd still live, try to do things, maintain my integrity through it. You know, that's it. Maybe I've found that my integrity is the most important thing, no matter what.

The changes in Hugh's life may appear fairly subtle to the observer, and the precipitating event might not be a trauma in the class of being disabled, going through combat, or the like. However, calling the prostitute was so foreign that it shook his view of the kind of person he was and it was emotionally distressing and threatening. In Hugh's case, this was necessary to set in motion the process of growth and to question the fundamental view of self, life priorities, and relating. For Hugh, these changes are not subtle at all—they are dramatic.

Session 13

Hugh: I'm going to New York next week for a job interview. And you know, I am completely confident.

Therapist: Different from how you've approached such situations before.

Hugh: Absolutely.

Therapist: I remember you telling me last time that you know your value now and your priorities.

Hugh: That's right. I am going to maintain my integrity, no matter what. I've lost the fear—that I wouldn't be accepted. Now I don't have to "show 'em." If they don't give me market value, you know what I'll say?

Therapist: What's that?

Hugh: I'll say, "You have a much greater task before you than I thought. To find someone who can do this job, who has a network in the industry to pull from, who can coordinate so many employees, and be responsible for a large chunk of the business, at the salary level you're talking." I'd wish them luck and leave with the confidence that I'll be employable elsewhere.

Therapist: Just when you stopped trying to show them, you *can* show them, although that's not relevant anymore.

Hugh: Before I was a weakling. Even though I would try hard to look good, I worried about whether I could pull it off, what if things went wrong. Now I just know I'll do what I can, and if it goes bad, it isn't me. I'm so thankful for what happened, but still so hate it. I hate what it did to Nancy. But without it I don't know if I would have seen this.

Therapist: You're free.

Hugh: To do what is me. I'm fearless. Even if I found out this biopsy is cancerous, I'd deal with it. I know there is an afterlife—I think back to those out-of-body experiences I had when I was young. Now I want to go on this interview to put this into action, then come back and report to you.

Session 14

Therapist: You went for your interview?

Hugh: Yeah, and my high school class reunion, too. Lots has happened.

Therapist: Tell me about it.

Hugh: I was at my class reunion, and was sitting with some people I really hadn't known well—it was a big class—and these folks were lawyers, executives, high-powered types. You know how we were talking last time about being free? Well, I was free there and had nothing to prove to them. I think I kind of surprised them with some things I said. Like I talked about changing jobs, and how I felt like I needed to do something that was more than just making more money for the company. And someone else started talking about thinking that same way. I even mentioned the out-of-body experiences that I had years ago and how that affected me spiritually. That's stuff I just don't say to people. And guess what? A couple other people at the table had similar things happen to them. Someone said that he respected me for being willing to talk about it. It was great conversation, and I felt so at ease. And the same for the interview. I had no fear—I even noticed when other people acted a bit nervous. I'd just wait calmly through some silly comment they made or whatever. I somehow wasn't concerned about how they saw me. Didn't need to "show 'em."

Therapist: Just as you had wanted to approach things.

Hugh: Now, here's a really amazing thing. I stayed in this hotel for $90 a night, and if you know New York, that's not a great place. So that section wasn't very good. I was coming home from dinner and a girl stopped me on the street—maybe she was in her early 20s. She said she wanted $5 for something to eat, and she'd do anything for me.

Therapist: So here's the test of whether you'd do something similar again.

Hugh: Not even close. I gave her the money and said, "the only thing you need to do is go get something to eat, and don't spend this foolishly, if you know what I mean." She was surprised, and said, you're so sweet, and hugged me and kissed me on the neck. And she said now she really wanted to go to bed with me. I told her that I wasn't going to take advantage of her, and that I wanted her to know that there were people who would really care about her. She said, "I don't see any." I told her she wouldn't see any where she hung out, but she could find people like that at social service agencies, churches, and so forth. And I did something else I just don't do, and told her I was a Christian, and that God was always there for her. It felt good and right.

Therapist: So different from before.

Hugh: I can hardly remember anymore what that was like before. How I felt about things. My whole attitude is changed. I really believe this transformation is permanent. I feel for the first time I am really me. I'm not having to keep up with lies. I'm free of those burdens. Trying to prove myself to others, I was putting myself in a one-down position right away. Now I take myself seriously, but I have humility, too. Intellectually I had known what I could do, but now I believe it, differently.

Therapist: It sounds like you've changed in ways that won't allow you to live on that old plane anymore—you're at a different level. From this new perspective, how are you viewing what you did with the other woman?

Hugh: This may sound strange, but I don't feel guilty about it like I did 2 months ago. If this needed to happen to change my life, so be it. But I don't know what happened here, in these sessions, what you did. I thought therapy was supposed to take 7 years.

Therapist: You think we are about done?

Hugh: It seems like it, unless you think there are other layers we have to peel back or something.

Therapist: You could always come back if you felt the need, but right now, it is hard to figure what you would need to do differently. Just nurture this way of living that is so satisfying to you.

Hugh: So you don't have a formula or something that you do with people.

Therapist: No. I think we've been a good match, and you were hurting bad enough that you were willing to really face things, face yourself. That makes a big difference.

Hugh: Well, I want you to know how grateful I am, how much this has meant to me.

It was tempting at times to jump at the things Hugh was saying and announce, "There it is—posttraumatic growth—don't you realize what's happening?!" It is still striking to us when clients, without any clear prompting from us, say things like, "it is the best of times and the worst of times" or "I feel enlightened." But we believe it is important to be quietly supportive and let clients marvel at the changes that are happening to them. That may well be sufficient without the additions of didactic instruction or academic explanations. Letting some mystery remain allows clients to continue to value this experience.

HAROLD: A LIFE REEXAMINED

Harold is a 48-year-old man who had lived an active, exciting, and often irresponsible life. He had been a photographer for many years, focusing on sports events, and had published pictures in many major publications. His photography had allowed him to get close to many celebrities and get invited to many parties. He had been a heavy drug user and drinker. He was divorced after 5 years of marriage after his wife became disenchanted with his lifestyle. She had been staying at home raising two children while Harold was on the road working and partying. After the divorce, he saw his children infrequently as he continued with his work. There was not a great difference in how he related to his family while he was married and after the divorce. He was generally inaccessible, although he thought of himself as a loving father.

Harold's son, David, was graduating from high school, and Harold was back home to be part of the festivities. Harold's son had struggled with asthma for years, and after the graduation ceremony at a family gathering he had a serious asthma attack. The family was quite knowledgeable about asthma and got David prompt attention at the hospital. However, David's condition worsened and he was dead 6 hours after the attack.

Harold struggled for several months to sort through his grief and continue to work, but he found it virtually impossible to go back on the road and pick up his old lifestyle. He stayed in his apartment printing pictures he had taken of David and isolated himself from other people. He began to run out of money, but didn't pay much attention to that. Finances no longer mattered in the aftermath of his son's death.

Harold presented himself for therapy about 7 months after David's death. For a couple of months, therapy had to do with recollections of David, Harold's attempts to find out what exactly happened that killed him, and his use of alcohol to medicate himself. Posttraumatic growth did not come quickly as it had with Hugh. However, after a series of sessions, Harold started to discuss the kind of father he had been to David.

Session 15

Harold: He was just graduating, and I was thinking of how I might be able to really start to show him around. How his mother might let him come with me more now that he was older. I was going to really be a father and we'd have a great time. I can't believe I won't get to do that. I always thought there would be time. Now I'm wondering if I really did much fathering at all. I mean, David always seemed to like me, but we didn't really know each other very well. Now it will never happen. (Crying) My only son ... I was never there for him ... I really blew it. I've been too wrapped up in myself. I thought I was a pretty cool Dad, but I wasn't a dad at all. I missed his whole life.

Therapist: It seems like you've been trying to be with him by printing all those pictures, remembering him to me in our sessions, and so forth.

Harold: What good does it do him. I never did him much good. I can't believe I didn't see all this before. What the hell is wrong with me?

Therapist: IS wrong or WAS wrong?

Harold: I sure do see things differently now. I wish I could go back and redo things.

Therapist: What would you do?

Harold: Oh, everything different. You know, Peggy gave me the message when we separated that I was a self-centered, irresponsible ass.

Couldn't see it then. She was right. Is this God's way of teaching me? Did God take my son to show me? Nothing else made a dent in me.

Therapist: I've never heard you mention anything about God before.

Harold: I always thought God was a bunch of crap. But now, I don't know. Nothing makes sense. None of this makes sense.

Therapist: You've been trying to make sense of all this?

Harold: Sort of, but it's all jumbled up. The only thing I know for sure is that I screwed up. I wasn't a father to David, and now he's dead. And I can't go back. And I have no interest in all that stuff I was doing. It's all so useless. Parties, pictures of people who think they're hot shit. Who cares?

Therapist: It sounds like the old ways just won't work for you anymore.

Harold: I could'nt care less.

Therapist: What are the new ways, then?

Harold: Who knows. Sitting in my place drinking, I guess. That sounds pretty stupid, too. I guess I only know how to live stupid.

Therapist: Do you want to learn how to live smart?

Harold: What's that? You know, I find myself wondering why live at all. Most of it is bullshit anyway.

Therapist: All that stuff that you used to think was so great, so much fun, that you were so good at, it's just bullshit?

Harold: Yup, I think so. I mean, I can't believe how this has hit me. I wonder if I ever really felt anything before.

Therapist: It's a hell of a thing to have to feel.

Harold: Yeah, but maybe it's good that I start to feel something. If I felt more back then, maybe I would have done different.

In this session, there are a number of growth themes that begin to emerge. The old ways of making sense of life, guiding decisions and actions, seem utterly useless. Harold begins to consider the value of responsibility, feeling, and even God. The therapist doesn't leap on any of this but just explores it. He asks Harold at one point about learning to live smart, a bit of a test of Harold's readiness to replace the old ways with some new principles. Harold's reply indicates that he's not quite ready for that and that he still has to dismantle the old ways, attack them. It is almost as if he takes his old schemas, or what is left of them, and stomps on them, making sure they are good and broken. He is angry with them for failing him.

In a subsequent session, Harold makes an announcement.

Session 17

Harold: Doc, I've stopped drinking. Threw all the stuff away. It just seemed stupid, and part of that stupid old life. I mean, before, I'd drink to party, and now I drink to feel lousy. I've got to stop doing both. I'm going to kill myself if I keep this up. Hell, I'll be homeless if I don't do something about work pretty soon. I never saved much, you know. But what is the point of someone like me living anyway?

Therapist: I guess you've figured there isn't much point to the old you living.

Harold: Right.

Therapist: It also sounds like the old you is disappearing. He can't be around without alcohol.

Harold: Right (Laughs). The old Harold always had to have some party juice ready. And other stuff, too, of course. But he's gone. It is so strange, I just can't imagine doing that stuff anymore. It's like foreign to me.

Therapist: To the new you.

Harold: Right. Maybe there is a new me.

Therapist: Who is he?

Harold: Don't know. Don't know him. All I know is he doesn't drink, or anything like that.

Therapist: It must be strange living with this new guy you don't know.

Harold: Yeah, but I think I'm looking forward to getting to know him. Or, maybe he doesn't even exist. Boy, this is a weird way to be talking!

Therapist: Everything has gotten pretty weird in the past few months, hasn't it?

Harold: You can say that again.

Session 19

In this session, Harold is clearer about how the old ways of living are in the past, but the new self-schema is undeveloped. This suggests a good metaphor to the therapist.

Therapist: You know, I was just thinking about what it is like when you develop pictures.

Harold: What do you mean?

Therapist: You know, how the images develop on the paper in the developing fluid.

Harold: Oh, yeah, I always like seeing that happen. Never tire of that. It's fun to see the photo take shape. Like magic.

Therapist: I was thinking that's what might be happening with the new you—taking shape gradually like that, and maybe some surprises there, too.

Harold: Yeah, at first, you wonder what you'll get. The negatives are really fun like that, seeing for the first time what you took.

Therapist: This process of learning about the new you may be a little like that.

Harold: Right, and I've got to play with it a little to make it look really good. Hey, right now, I've cropped booze right out of the picture!

At this point in treatment, it seems almost inevitable that posttraumatic growth is happening and will continue. The therapist judiciously introduces encouragement and focuses on this process, but does not demand any growth. Instead, the clinician works best by noticing it—saying to the client in different ways—look at that! The therapist also makes subtle reference to the future. In the case of Harold, the therapist used the photography metaphor to suggest that developments will be forthcoming. The photographer can readily appreciate this, having experiences that he can draw on to extend the metaphor himself. The general feeling about it is excitement, and this suggests that these feelings can be part of the posttrauma experience as well.

Session 22

Harold: I've been thinking about God again. You know, I've just assumed David's in heaven, and it has hit me that I must then believe in God in some way. And if that is the case … well, I don't know. It has some sort of implications, I guess. I just can't not believe that David still lives spiritually. That there is a heaven for him.

Therapist: You've never had to give much thought to these things before.

Harold: But now they are really important. And I'm surprised about what I do believe. And now where does that leave me? If there is a God, then what? Am I supposed to live a certain way?

Therapist: I remember you saying before that you were wondering if God had David die to show you how to live.

Harold: Yeah, I know, but I don't think I really believe that. I don't go for the idea that God punishes people like that. But I guess I don't know much about God at all. Strangely enough, I'm interested in finding out though.

Therapist: Finding out about God?

Harold: Yeah. But I can't see me going to church or anything. I was thinking about reading some stuff.

Therapist: Scripture?

Harold: Oh, I don't know if I could make sense of the Bible or anything. I don't know, this is crazy for me. This new me is a weird guy!

Therapist: Harold, it seems to me that this new you isn't quite so distraught.

Harold: That's true. I seem to be on some kind of mission. You know what I did?

Therapist: What?

Harold: I sent Peggy and Shelly (his 16-year-old daughter) some pictures of David. I mean, really terrific pictures. I blew up stuff I had taken years ago; I took some of the things I'd been obsessively printing in the past few months and made kind of a book of David.

Therapist: That sounds wonderful.

Harold: Yeah. It came out great. Shelly loves it. But Peggy says she just can't look at it. But I think she'll like it someday.

In this session, Harold is seriously considering his spiritual life. Instead of being an absolute atheist, he recognizes himself as having some spiritual dimension, although unexplored and poorly informed. He mentions he is on a mission and tells about one part of his mission, giving the photographs to his ex-wife and daughter. What seemed to be aimless activity in the past (printing photos obsessively) has been made purposeful. It is sometimes not necessary for clinicians to label everything that is happening to the client. We have come to have great faith in this process of unfolding change and posttraumatic growth so that we don't feel we need to take extraordinary steps to further it. In fact, sometimes, by being too direct about it, the mystical quality of it can be spoiled. There is much to be said for letting this process remain somewhat mystical for the trauma survivor. The affective element in the experience tends to be stronger this way, and that seems important in the continuing development of posttraumatic growth. Returning to Harold again, consider another theme that emerges in one of the final sessions with him.

Session 25

Harold: Shelly's been calling me some since I sent her the book of David. She asks me about the pictures, especially the ones when he was little, things she can't remember.

Therapist: It's different for her to be in touch like this?

Harold: Oh, yeah. She's never had much to say to me. Like she's always ticked off a little. But you, know, I still have a daughter, and I can put up with some of that. I'm just going to be some kind of father to her.

Therapist: Some kind?

Harold: It's hard from a distance, and I'm not sure at this point she wants anything from me.

Therapist: But she is calling.

Harold: That's right. So something's going on. You know I have a peaceful feeling, that Shelly and I will work things out. You can tell she really misses her brother, and I feel sorry for her. Peggy, too. I can tell she's really suffering. I've hesitated to tell her what I've been going through. I thought she'd say, "What are you grieving for? You've never been around all these years." But she hasn't been like that at all. In fact when I told her how hard this has hit me, she was very kind about it. When I told her I felt guilty about not being there, she wasn't really very comforting, though. She said, "What can I say? I'm sure you know how I feel about that." I can't blame her, it's okay. We've actually been in touch more since David's death than before. A lot of business stuff, but also just talking. She is a good person. I feel like apologizing to her, but it would seem hollow.

Therapist: It sounds like this grief has softened everyone up a bit

Harold: Yeah. I don't feel like defending myself. And I see what they're going through, and I'd like to do something, it just doesn't seem to be my place, after all this time.

Therapist: So you sent the pictures.

Harold: It was something I could do.

Therapist: This is different for you?

Harold: Yes, my feelings are driving me. That's different.

Therapist: So what do you think?

Harold: (Softly) I think it's good.

Changes in ways of relating and the development of empathy and compassion are evident here. Again, the therapist in this instance doesn't have to do much but point out in very brief comments the changes that are already in progress. The client's labels are often good enough. Harold says, "My feelings are driving me" and "it's good." When the astute, empathic therapist can tell this is clearly recognized, he can let it be. We hope to make clear in subsequent chapters that posttraumatic growth therapy is subtle. The therapist's stance is that this natural tendency in the trauma survivor is to be nurtured, not created by the therapist. The therapist may notice seeds that will later germinate into posttraumatic growth, but must be patient for the conditions to be right for the germination. With Harold, some of the seeds from earlier sessions started to sprout a few weeks later.

Most of the time, our clients have stumbled into posttraumatic growth without any sense they were doing anything than merely struggling to survive. However, we have encountered some survivors who at some point have said to us, "The pain is too great for nothing good to come of this." They then proceeded to make the good.

3

The Process of Encouraging
Posttraumatic Growth: An Overview

What can the clinician do to increase the likelihood that a client will experience posttraumatic growth? The easy answer is, be a good clinician. Within the parameters delineated by *good clinician*, however, there are some matters that are specific to posttraumatic growth that are useful to introduce before we begin a discussion of encouraging the discovery of growth in each of the separate domains of posttraumatic growth. This chapter examines some general guidelines that result primarily from our personal experiences as clinicians. It is important to regard these suggestions as fluid and open to change as the research on posttraumatic growth continues and suggests alternative approaches.

COMMON PRINCIPLES OF CONTEMPORARY
TRAUMA TREATMENT

Facilitation of posttraumatic growth can be accomplished within the general framework of trauma treatment, either by implementing the principles we describe within those treatments or adding this piece of treatment after the primary work of trauma therapy has been substantially accomplished. Some treatment programs make mention of facilitation of growth (e.g., Meichenbaum, 1994), but most are not explicit in this regard. We recognize that there are a variety of therapeutic approaches to trauma that have been described based on varying theoretical principles, individual, group, inpatient, outpatient, brief, and long-term treatment. Although there is danger in oversimplification here, we mention the common therapeutic strategies that we notice in various trauma treatments.

Essential to trauma treatment is desensitization. Because the events surrounding the trauma and what has become associated with it provoke anxiety in the form of exaggerated startle responses, hypervigilance and the like, and avoidance responses that have both behavioral and cognitive elements, desensitization is a common aspect of all trauma treatment. This is accomplished through exposure to the trauma in detailed descriptions or thinking of traumatic events in conjunction with a safe therapeutic atmosphere, directed eye movements, hypnotic or relaxation procedures, and so on. Of course psychopharmacological interventions are often useful in alleviating many of these symptoms.

A second element has to do with creating a narrative that makes sense of the incidents or at least understandable in some basic way. Because traumas are often poorly encoded in memory, a narrative serves the purpose of linking together elements of the traumatic memories, speculations about motives of those involved, and other poorly understood aspects of the trauma so that the survivor has a good enough model to refer to in recovery. The trauma survivor must have some degree of clarity about what they are recovering from.

A third element has to do with re-creating a sense of safety. Developing the therapeutic alliance can serve this purpose. Networking with other trauma survivors can also play a role in finding some degree of safety in the world. Of course some trauma survivors utilize inpatient treatments to discover a sense of safety again. Therapists usually work with their clients on self-protective strategies that can allow a trauma survivor to feel less vulnerable to revictimization.

A final element has to do with re-creating a worldview that encompasses what happened as well as a functional life posttrauma. To some extent, this aspect of trauma treatment is involved in the construction of the narrative that describes the trauma and provides some understanding of it. This view also allows for a more hopeful stance toward the future, including how a survivor could be free of their distressing symptoms, how life might be possible without revictimization, and how meaning and purpose are still possible.

A NEW PERSPECTIVE—NOT A NEW
TREATMENT METHOD

The focus in this book is on the process of posttraumatic growth and the possible role that clinicians can play in making it more likely. This is neither a proposal for a new school of psychotherapy nor a particular approach to treating persons in crisis. What we have to say can be applied by clinicians working within a variety of theoretical frameworks with clients who have experienced a wide range of highly stressful situations. The book represents an attempt to provide clinicians with a different perspective on traumatic events. Quite justifiably, the major thrust of the clinical and research work on the aftermath of trauma has focused on how individuals can be affected negatively. As was seen in chapter 1, the possible negative consequences of highly stressful events are plentiful.

However, as individuals struggle to manage, survive, and come to terms with the tragedies and losses of their lives, many can experience a variety of changes that they view as positive and even as overwhelmingly good. The exclusive focus on the need to identify and address the negative consequences of trauma may lead clinicians inadvertently to overlook the possibility that some, and perhaps many, individuals can experience positive change in the wake of tragedy and loss. Clinicians may want to adopt a new perspective—the possibility exists that individuals can be changed for the better by their struggle with crisis.

IS IT POSSIBLE FOR THE CLINICIAN
TO CREATE GROWTH?

It is important to remember that there is a limit to the degree to which psychotherapy can produce changes in clients (Mahoney, 1991). Counselors, particularly those who are just beginning their work, must remind themselves that although the work can be deeply rewarding, the task of helping individuals who have been exposed to extremely difficult situations is difficult and challenging. The work that clinicians do can help many clients change in positive ways. However, some clients may not be helped at all; for others, the clinician must be prepared to regard even small changes as success. How much difference can clinicians make in the client's posttraumatic growth?

At a conference presentation, one of us (LGC) commented that he tended to believe that clinicians could probably not do anything to create growth for the client. After the session was over, a trauma therapist who had been in the audience came up, noticeably distressed, and asked: "Do you really believe that we are that powerless with our clients? I think that there is a lot we can do!" In retrospect, both the presenter and the clinician in the audience were right. There are certainly a variety of clinical attitudes, perspectives, and behaviors that are more likely to encourage growth in clients. However, it seems unlikely that the clinician can independently construct growth for the client, *give* growth, or teach it in some structured, didactic fashion. The clinician can help the client achieve growth and can encourage growth, but the clinician cannot make growth for the client.

We are not saying anything that good clinicians do not already know: The most effective interventions are those that lead the client to independently utilize his or her own abilities to successfully cope with difficulties. In the domain of posttraumatic growth, the clinician can create a therapeutic context where the client can develop in positive ways, but growth is something only the client can achieve. There is probably not much chance of the clinician creating growth out of nothing for the client, but there will be opportunities to help the client find growth when it has the potential to occur. Although expectations must be realistic, it is also important for the clinician to always be open to the possibility of major and radical positive change in the client.

Although there are circumstances where growth is clearly reflected in observable changes in behavior, a major way in which individuals experience posttraumatic growth is in a shift of life paradigms (Tedeschi & Calhoun, 1995). Recall that chapter 1 described posttraumatic growth as occurring in the domains of changed philosophy of life, a changed sense of relationships with others, and a changed sense of self. Changes in any of these areas can be reflected in changed behavior. Regardless of whether change is observable externally, the individual may experience change internally in any of these areas. For example, the woman whose miscarriage makes her more sensitive to similar losses in other women may experience greater compassion. Her experience of their losses may be significantly different compared with her reaction before her own loss. This changed experience is positive for her. However, others may not be able to readily observe that she is reacting or she is doing anything differently.

PROCESSES FOR ENCOURAGING POSTTRAUMATIC GROWTH

Respect and Work Within the Client's Framework

Clinicians in every profession have some training in the skill of accurately understanding the client's internal world (i.e., the process of empathy). The clinician must understand the client's general worldview and belief system. To enhance the possibility of posttraumatic growth, the clinician also must work within the client's framework. One specific area involves the acceptance and tolerance of *positive illusions* (Taylor & Brown, 1994). There is some evidence indicating that human beings tend to operate with certain *benign illusions* (Taylor, 1989). In general, people tend to have somewhat positively biased views of themselves, their ability to control events, and the likelihood that the future will provide many blessings but few curses. For example, when asked how they compare with other people, a large majority of respondents usually indicate that they are above average. When working with clients in the aftermath of trauma, clinicians may find themselves confronting benign illusions about positive ways their clients assume they have changed. The clinician must be willing to tolerate, and work with, points of view of the client that the clinician may regard as having illusory elements. Some therapists may be reluctant to do this because they worry that accepting or acknowledging the client's description of the experience of growth may be the same as encouraging denial.

An important consideration for the clinician is what the response should be if the client's conceptualizations do appear to involve denial. To be able to say accurately that the client is *in denial* requires that the clinician have knowledge of what the reality is and also knowledge that the client is incapable of consciously accepting that reality. The theoretical assumption is that the individual's inability to accept reality serves the adaptive function of keeping overwhelmingly anxious elements out of awareness. Even if the clinician has clear evidence that the client is utilizing the defense mechanism of denial, it is crucial to remember that defense mechanisms are psychologically protective. The precipitous and ill-considered effort directly to eliminate such defenses may well produce high levels of distress for the client. In addition, however, the client's denial of empirically confirmable elements of traumatic events is likely to be the exception rather than the rule in the everyday practice of most therapists. Although certainly possible, denial and repression are less typical than the intrusion and reexperiencing of traumatic elements. Clinicians may still wonder about the advisability of the client's conceptualizations even in situations similar to those where a sports referee would be required to make a judgment call. In circumstances where the information available to the therapist does not clearly and unambiguously contradict the client's point of view, we recommend that the clinician accept and work within the client's understanding of the situation.

For example, a client construes his or her new identity in the posttraumatic struggle as reflecting stronger religious faith and deeper spirituality. In contrast, the clinician sees no such thing. In fact, the clinician's perception is that if anything the client's faith is weaker and religion less important. How should the clinician respond to this incongruity? Isn't the client in denial? Shouldn't the therapist confront the client? This is clearly a judgment call because it would be difficult or impossible for the clinician to collect information that would allow the spirituality issue to be decided with empirical evidence. In addition, the use of the term *denial* to describe a defense mechanism used to control anxiety seems questionable in this instance. In these kinds of situations, it is recommended that the clinician continue to work within the perspective that the client has developed.

Of course clinicians should not ignore psychotic delusions or accept unethical behavior. Rather, within the parameters dictated by common sense and good ethics, the pursuit of absolute empirical truth is not always a worthwhile endeavor when working with clients dealing with the aftermath of trauma. Because much of posttraumatic growth is likely to be internal and experiential, some clients may report experiencing positive changes for which the clinician sees no corroborating behavioral evidence. For example, a client reports that, because of his own suffering, he is now much more sympathetic to others who experience loss, yet there is no noticeable change in how he treats other people in his own cancer support group. How should the clinician respond to this particular positive illusion? It will be useful for the therapist to allow or encourage the client to talk about his renewed sense of sympathy with others who suffer. The clinician should inquire how this experience of sympathy is affecting his or her life and where this change may lead, but direct confrontation and destruction of the client's benign illusions is usually undesirable.

Our suggestion is that, in general, even if the clinician views the client's experience of positive change as illusory, the clinician should tolerate and respect the client's perception. To work effectively in this area, the clinician must be willing to tolerate some degree of positive illusions because such toleration increases the chances for the client to cope more effectively. In addition, the client's real experience of growth may be reflected in those illusions.

A subset of the individual's general worldview that may also require some flexibility on the part of the clinician is the individual's spiritual or religious views. These matters are discussed in more detail in chapter 6, but an early reminder is appropriate. For many individuals, an important arena of posttraumatic growth is in existential or religious matters. To effectively encourage growth in these areas, clinicians must be comfortable when clients raise issues in this area; they must also be capable of actively engaging the individual who experiences growth occurring in the spiritual or religious sphere.

Early Stages of Treatment

In the early stages of treatment with an individual who has recently experienced a highly traumatic event, the discussion of growth is usually premature. In the beginning, the development of the therapeutic relationship, the management of acute psychological distress, and the client's experience of safety are primary goals (Herman, 1992). As the summary in chapter 1 suggested, there are multiple ways in which individuals can experience negative physical and psychological consequences of traumatic events. It is typical for individuals to feel high levels of distress, and significant psychological impairment is possible. The greater the degree to which the life crisis includes threats to the individual's life, exposure to horrible events, or major catastrophe, the greater the possibility that early treatment needs to focus on simply assisting the client to cope and manage day to day. As Herman (1992), suggested "The first principle of recovery is the empowerment of the survivor." (p. 133)

For most clinicians in general practice, however, the problems clients face are more likely to be reasonably common life crises that do shake the foundations of the individuals' worldview, but may not necessarily involve intensely traumatic sets of events. Nevertheless, in the early stages of intervention, it is important for the psychotherapist to focus on helping the client to make the level of psychological distress manageable. There are multiple therapeutic avenues available for clinicians to follow in helping clients deal with traumatic events and life crises. Regardless of the specific theoretical perspective or therapeutic program that clinicians employ, we think that early on the focus needs to be on helping the client reduce psychological pain and initiate the process of coping, surviving, and eventual recovery.

However, the clinician must beware of approaches to intervention that stifle the possibility of growth by smothering all distress. There is a fine line between helping the client manage distress and assisting the client to contemplate and mull over, which the traumatic event sets in motion. We are not suggesting that the counselor work to maintain pain where relief is possible. However, for growth to be possible, the individual needs to have support for the rumination process set in motion by the life crisis, which allows for positive change. It is best to think about posttraumatic growth as something that unfolds over time, rather than as something that individuals develop in an intense flash of instant insight. The clinician must be open to the possibility of growth from the very beginning of the work with an individual client, but there must also be a general assumption that growth is something that unfolds over the longer term.

There are varying routes to growth. As discussed in chapter 2, a client like Hugh can begin to show some posttraumatic growth in the first few sessions. Hugh had already been in a distressing life situation, and his own behavior produced the crisis that in turn prompted a consideration of changes. The preexisting distress may lead people like Hugh to seize on their crises and convert them rapidly into opportunities for growth and change. In Hugh's case, there was still much rumination to do, but the growth became evident early on. One thing that helped him was that he and his wife reconciled; this relieved a great deal of distress and preoccupation, perhaps allowing for consideration of growth. In sessions, he would talk about the internal struggle between wanting to move on from all that had happened and the determination to continue to confront himself with his behavior and mine his mistake for its value. For other people, the growth process is considerably longer. We have found that intense psychic pain must be relieved for the possibility of growth to become apparent, but enduring distress maintains a kind of rumination—the more deliberate kind—that is central to the process of posttraumatic growth. Given the experiences of some trauma survivors, much time and work may be necessary to relieve the intense psychic pain.

Past Traumas

When clients seek help dealing with the aftermath of a recent crisis, they often raise issues related to past traumatic experiences. The current problems can reactivate unresolved issues connected to past difficulties, but old crises can also provide a fruitful source for recognizing growth that the individual has already experienced. As the client talks about past crises, how they reacted, and what the aftermath has been, there may be opportunities for the clinician to help the client process manifestations of posttraumatic growth. A 23-year-old man who, because of a divorce, had become the single parent of a 2-year-old child sought treatment because he had recently experienced a recurrence of his substance abuse problems. He had moderate symptoms of clinical depression and described a highly stressful set of current life circumstances: He had almost no friends, was solely responsible for the care of his daughter, his financial circumstances were marginal, and there was a chance that he would soon lose his job. In the first session, he recounted how it had been a great struggle for him to bring himself to separate from his wife. He had made the choice primarily based on his wife's unwillingness to seek help for her severe and long-standing substance dependence. Given his rather timid and unassertive interpersonal style, it was clear that having initiated the process of separating from a spouse had required an immense effort on his part, but he had done it "because it was clear that was the thing that my daughter needed."

His current difficulties were only indirectly connected to his separation. However the client's description of his past encounter with crisis provided the clinician with an opportunity to help him recognize and label the degree to which his actions reflected the utilization of skills and strengths that, before the birth of his child, he had not fully recognized in himself. This also illustrates why posttraumatic growth may be difficult for some clients to recognize. This young man utilized a self-schema that did not easily allow for accessing any thought of himself as capable. The clinician's job is to help the client construct a new set of beliefs about self using the evidence of adaptive coping with trauma; this allows the client to more readily utilize this view of self in coping with future difficulties. This can be fairly tedious work, as the clinician repeats this message to the client: "I've noticed something in you that you tend to overlook in yourself."

The clinician can encourage this process by supporting the client in a thorough and complete telling of the events surrounding the trauma and perhaps also of the individual's life before. The telling of the story can drain away some of the emotional impact over time, but it may be experienced as distressing during the process itself. Therefore, the clinician must be attuned to the client's readiness to enter back into the trauma memories and not demand this. However, the personal description of the events and the individual's responses can provide a context for the identification of changes experienced as growth. Clinical intervention may best be viewed as a continual process of narrative development, where the events and experiences are revisited and retold many times, with new details included in each version, and different perspectives are taken on the same events. As new details and perceptions are included in each version, the aftermath of the crisis is revisited by each telling. For many individuals, the retelling will gradually begin to include elements of posttraumatic growth. For example, in a group meeting of bereaved parents, a newly bereaved couple joined, prompting a retelling of the circumstances of their children's deaths by each family represented in the group. After a particular mother told the story of her son's death, several group members remarked about how differently she told it this time compared to the first time about 4 months earlier. One group member said, "This time you included all the details of what had happened the day before, all the precious times you had that day. You didn't tell us about that before. It's like that's part of it now, too, not just the horror."

Later Stages

Perhaps one of the later manifestations of posttraumatic growth is the client's ability to describe it to oneself and to others. The weaving of the trauma into the fabric of the individual's life narrative is not as easy as it may seem. It can require work over an extended period of time. However, until survivors of a major life crisis can successfully construct meaningful personal narratives that organize the information about themselves (McAdams, 1993) and the trauma, growth may be experienced only as ephemeral and tentative. The client is much farther along when he or she is able to notice growth patterns without the clinician highlighting them. We saw this in Hugh's case in chapter 2. When he could describe himself as *enlightened*, he was more confident that the changes he was experiencing would be lasting.

Aspects of the Process of Encouraging Growth

One purpose of this book is to provide some general ways of approaching work with persons who have experienced major life stress—ranging from the extremely traumatic on the one hand to the less dramatic but nevertheless distressing on the other hand. Because of the wide range of specific kinds of problems that clients bring to treatment, we purposefully avoid making excessively specific prescriptions. We provide some rather specific steps in later chapters, but even they must be applied to specific persons with a significant amount of good clinical judgment. This section addresses some general matters that are highly specific to the work of helping clients with posttraumatic growth.

Focus on Listening, Without Necessarily Trying to Solve.   This suggestion applies to clinical work that will typically occur after the initial stages of treatment have helped reduce distress and have led to some satisfactory coping. Some approaches to crisis intervention and the treatment of posttraumatic stress syndromes are highly structured and directive (Jaycox, Foa, & Morral, 1998), whereas others are less directive and structured (Herman, 1992; McCann & Pearlman, 1990). To enhance the likelihood that posttraumatic growth is experienced, it is important for the clinician to cultivate the ability to be fully present with the client. This requires the clinician to have a substantial degree of comfort enduring the telling of sometimes horrific stories. The response of the clinician should be quietly sympathetic, without disturbing the telling, and without usurping the affect the client has in response to his or her experiences. Unfortunately, some clinicians give quite definite personal reactions to the stories that are told; we recommend quiet, but clear presence.

Some clinicians also feel a need to provide a solution for the client, or at least to engage actively in some process that will be useful to the client. We felt this as beginning clinicians ourselves and we see it frequently in the beginning clinicians we train. The temptation is to provide at least some expertise, give helpful advice or suggestions, or offer what amounts to a psychological equivalent of the written prescription the physician hands to the patient. Experienced clinicians are not immune to this temptation; and in some contexts, this felt need can lead to helpful therapeutic exchanges. For the process of psychotherapy to assist the client to experience elements of posttraumatic growth, however, it may be better for the clinician to adopt the general stance that is suggested by a Buddhist saying: "Don't just do something— sit there." When working with clients who have experienced life crises, the clinician must adopt an attitude of listening to the accounts and narratives that the client develops. It is within those accounts that the experience of posttraumatic growth may be most visible to the clinician. This clinical stance also provides the basis for a thorough examination of the effects of trauma on fundamental beliefs and how the client perceives the self and the world, rather than purely on distress relief. The clinician adopts the implicit view of trauma with the client: "I'm sorry you went through this, but now how can we respond in a way that is useful and strengthens you?" Again, the clinician may never say this directly, but in showing respect for the trauma survivors experience, there is communicated the possibility that it could be used in some way that is ultimately of value to the client.

In an earlier book (Tedeschi & Calhoun, 1995), we chose two quotes that illustrate the power of this kind of listening for both the client and the therapist. To us, they remain excellent examples of the stance the clinician takes in promoting posttraumatic growth. First, a pediatric oncologist describes the response of an adolescent patient to her willingness to be still and present:

> For an agonizing hour he poured out his young-ancient soul. Then he rose from the chair with tears pouring down his face. "You're the best doctor I've ever met," he exclaimed. "No one has ever helped me as much as you have. How can I thank you?" I had never gotten to say a word to Jay. I had only listened. (Komp, 1993, p. 62)

In describing trauma treatment of Vietnam veterans, another therapist makes the same point:

> The advice that veterans consistently give to trauma therapists is "Listen! Just listen." Respect, embodied in this kind of listening, is readiness to be changed by the narrator. The change may be small or large. It may be simply learning something not previously known, feeling something, seeing something from a new perspective, or it may be as profound as redirection of the listener's way of being in the world. (Shay, 1994, p. 189)

This is an especially radical view of the therapy process, one that is the foundation of working toward posttraumatic growth in trauma survivors. Therapists must listen in a way that allows themselves to be changed, rather than be intent on doing the changing. The way to approach therapy with this group is to be open to the possibility of learning from the client in a way that is emotionally as well as intellectually satisfying. Go into the session being open to both the distress and the possibility. Feel privileged to be on this journey with this survivor for whom survival was once the only goal, but who now sees other developments as well and who is willing to explore these surprising aspects of survival.

Notice Growth as the Client Approaches It. Perhaps the single most important message of this book is for the clinician to be able to perceive posttraumatic growth as the client begins to consider this possibility. The possibility of posttraumatic growth is revealed primarily, although not exclusively, in verbal exchanges. If the clinician wants to help the client discover posttraumatic growth, then the clinician must first be prepared to listen and bring into focus growth that is implicit in the client's account. Much of what is important is expressed beneath the words; the clinician must be open to this kind of communication to identify movement toward posttraumatic growth. This way of attending to clients was recognized long ago by Theodor Reik in his description of "listening with the third ear." What the client says "dives down into the unconscious mind of the psychologist" (Reik, 1948, p. 131). True understanding of the client can only happen when the emotional life of the clinician is open to the stories of the client. Getting beyond the specific meaning of words to see the larger pattern of struggle toward growth demands an emotionally open stance on the part of the clinician. The cognitive psychologist Kelly (1969) made a similar point when he directed therapists to:

> listen primarily to the subcortical sounds and themes that run through his client's talk. Stop wondering what words literally mean ... think of these vocal sounds, not as words, but as preverbal outcries, impulsive sound gestures, stylized oral grimaces, or hopelessly mumbled questions. (p. 229)

We have found that the struggle to understand what a trauma will do to one's life, how life can be in the aftermath, and the distress of not believing or even understanding things are all positive signs that growth may occur. Clinicians can recognize this distressing struggle as more than merely a posttraumatic response, but as the precursor to growth.

At the same time, it is important not to short-circuit the client's struggle or act as a growth expert. The client must still take the journey.

Label It When It Is There. Acknowledge and reinforce the experience of growth when it is articulated by the client, but not prematurely. Reinforce the reasonable positive interpretations of growth coming from the struggle with trauma when the client makes them. As noted earlier, remember that the clinician may want to explicitly label growth that is only implicit in the client's narrative. To do this appropriately requires tact and sensitivity on the part of the clinician. The clinician responds to what the client presents as elements of growth that are beginning to be incorporated into the individual's account of the event or in the broader narrative of his or her life. This can be done by labeling changes that the client identifies as already present, but that have not been explicitly identified as such, or by reframing the way the individual views certain events.

For example, a man sought help after some weeks of high levels of joint pain that had culminated in the diagnosis of a chronic, recurrently painful arthritic condition. There was no cure for the disease, and it tended to flare up following prolonged periods of physical activity. Because his work involved high levels of activity, he was forced to reduce the number of hours he worked and accept payments for partial disability. He was generally depressed by the irreversibility of his condition as well as the pain. In his first session, he had indicated that part of his reason for seeking help was an interest in marriage counseling because he and his wife had "not gotten along for some time." In a later session, he commented that over the past "couple of weeks" things had been much better. He reported that his wife was "being really solicitous with me and real supportive, and I am starting to realize that maybe I have underestimated her"; in turn he was starting to "appreciate the stuff she has done for me over the past few months." The clinician responded by indicating that "it sounds like one of the things you are discovering is that, at least in some ways, your illness and discomfort have served to bring the two of you a little closer together." The clinician's response allowed the client to identify and label a change that had elements of potential posttraumatic growth in an important personal relationship.

However, the clinician must guard against offering platitudes about what wonderful opportunities crises are (Calhoun & Tedeschi, 1991). The goal is to listen well and carefully to the whole story of the survivor, with all its components—affective, cognitive, and behavioral. As clinicians listen and observe carefully, they can provide support to clients as they begin to articulate the experience of positive change as it emerges in the wake of a major life crisis. Sometimes what might seem like a platitude at one point is clearly acceptable at another. Therefore, the clinician must make sure that any attempts to reinforce, label, or bring growth into focus for the client are timed well. We have found in our work that the immediate aftermath of a traumatic set of circumstances is not a good time to focus on posttraumatic growth. It is essential that the timing of actions designed to enhance growth occur in the overall context of the individual client's experience and the events he or she has encountered. There will be circumstances where some clients may approach the issue of growth, but clinicians should be careful not to leap on these too quickly.

Particularly when dealing with events that are still overwhelming to the client, the focus needs to be on helping the client survive and manage basic coping tasks. This is clearly the case when the events are those that put individuals at risk for posttraumatic syndromes. For example, it may be quite a long time, if ever, that a young woman who is sexually abused can see any good coming out of her struggle with that negative set of circumstances. Posttraumatic growth can happen, in some ways, for some people who are victimized like this (Herman, 1992), but it would be a mistake to assume that posttraumatic growth always happens.

When the events involve major personal losses, such as the death of an infant, or the events are repellent and incomprehensible (e.g., the Holocaust), the client may interpret the experience of growth as a sign of disloyalty or a lack of moral principle. In these instances, the clinician must be extremely sensitive about when, or even if, to identify or label the occurrence of posttraumatic growth. The individual may experience distress or revulsion at even the possibility that they could see growth arising from their struggle with that particular loss. Even when the events are tragic, our suggestion is that the counselor remain attuned to the possibility of growth. When the proper therapeutic relationship is in place, and if the client's own account provides evidence that growth is occurring, it is useful to gradually bring it into focus for the client.

In a support group for grieving parents, the mother of a toddler who had died in a motor vehicle accident had alluded several times to her recommitment to work with homeless children. Her involvement in volunteer work at the local shelter was motivated, at least in part, by her wish to prevent other mothers from going through the despair that she had experienced with the death of her child. During the third group session, in which she alluded to her volunteer work, one of the group's co-leaders remarked that the client's own loss had led her to be motivated to spare other parents the kind of pain she was feeling. The mother's initial reaction was one of immediate anger. "You know, I think I could have figured that out without Joey dying!" Fortunately, in the next session, her view was slightly different; she indicated that she guessed that in fact her own despair and pain had moved her into a good direction that she might not otherwise have been moved.

Events That Are Too Horrible. Are not some events simply so horrible that it is a repellent notion that any good at all, ever, could come from the struggle with them? This is a question that only the individual affected can answer, but the data on posttraumatic growth may give some helpful guidance. Although the percentages of persons who report growth vary with different situations, and although the extent of the growth experienced varies widely from person to person, the research suggests that at least some people experience some growth from the struggle with even the most horrible events imaginable (Tedeschi & Calhoun, 1995). In considering findings that persons with disabilities often have more positive views about their circumstances than observers of their conditions, Wright (1989), made an important point about the distinction between the traumatic event or condition, which may be horrible, and its "ramifying meaning" that survivors may value.

> The point is, however, that appreciating a disability, giving it value, need not require that it be preferred in and of itself; just that its ramifying meaning is valued. Consider how often there is a strong positive reaction to a person who refuses to succumb to the limitations of a disability and instead is challenged to overcome and achieve. It is then that the disability, being viewed within a broader life context of a dauntless human spirit, becomes appreciated for what it signifies. Nevertheless, because the notion of disability is typically viewed in isolation from any valued context, such positive embedding will probably remain elusive in the way most people generally orient themselves to the meaning of disability. (p. 528)

Hence, clinicians need to be open to the possibility of growth, and it may be that our clients may be better at recognizing it than we are. We should always follow the lead provided by the clients' experiences and their descriptions of those experiences. Clinicians can check out clients' willingness to think in terms of posttraumatic growth by saying, "Some people I've worked with have said that they have changed in some positive ways as they coped with their trauma. Do you think that is possible for you, given the kinds of things you went through?" Although many clients will provide evidence of posttraumatic growth, we caution clinicians once again that posttraumatic growth is neither inevitable nor universal.

Choosing the Right Words. The words that clinicians choose to label or identify posttraumatic growth are important. It may have become redundantly obvious that we have studiously avoided talking about the events that trigger growth. When talking with clients, the word choice needs to reflect that the growth is not produced by the event (e.g., the death of a 2-year-old child), but by the individual's struggle to survive and come to terms with what has happened. One of the reasons that Joey's mother, described earlier, became so angry at the clinician co-leading the group was that his word choice was unfortunate. Although he had accurately perceived some elements of posttraumatic growth in the woman's experience, what he said was, "It seems that Joey's death has led you to be more committed to helping others avoid your kind of pain." In our view, it would have been more advisable if the focus had been placed on the woman's *struggle* with the loss of her son, rather than on the son's death. Simply changing the phrase slightly would have been desirable: "Your struggle with the pain produced by Joey's loss has led you to be more committed to helping others avoid your kind of pain." We do not know if the woman's response was solely the result of the phrasing or of the belief that perceiving growth would be experienced by her as a betrayal of Joey. However, the example suggests that clinicians should be most judicious in the way they choose to reflect, label, or highlight growth that has occurred as a result of the individual's struggle to cope.

The Helpful Role of Groups

The general framework we adopt in this book is that of one clinician working with one client. However, group settings also provide unique and helpful means for the development of posttraumatic growth. In fact, when survivors of traumas gather, they often assign more credibility to each other than to clinicians who lead such groups. These group members can say things that leaders cannot, including noticing growth outcomes. However, group members may be oblivious to such outcomes and may need prompting by a leader. As mentioned earlier referring to the reports of other survivors can be a strategy that allows group members to consider growth possibilities: "I've heard some bereaved parents say that they have changed in some ways that they value as a result of coping with their child's death. Have you noticed anything like that?"

Over several years of facilitating bereaved parent support groups, one of the authors (RGT) heard many reports of posttraumatic growth offered spontaneously by group members. Often it is unnecessary to even comment on these reports. They are striking enough to stand on their own without embellishment. For example, one father who had lost a 12-year-old daughter described how her death changed the way he coached little league. He couldn't bear to see kids hurt and changed his philosophy from win at almost any cost. He described his new approach as "everyone gets to learn the skills, play and try them out, and have a good time without worry that they will be taken out of the game." He thought he had become a wiser coach who saw the influence he could have on the children in his charge, rather than being focused on winning as much as possible. The clinician could have embellished this report by citing other ways this man clearly had become more tender and compassionate. However, at this point, it seemed that acknowledging his change in coaching philosophy was significant enough for this man. Maybe later he would be able to see this as part of his revised philosophy of life.

Perhaps the greatest benefit of therapy in groups for posttraumatic growth is the discussion of perspective, offering of beliefs, and the use of metaphor to explain experience. All of this is fertile ground for the revision of schemas that is essential to the experience of growth. This is best done in a way that no one is on the spot and members can simply consider the ways that others construe things and try on these possibilities. Leaders or facilitators make the potential for growth more salient by inviting talk about change and perspective. Questions along the lines of "What changes have you noticed in yourself since this happened?" and "How do you make sense of this?" are useful in encouraging this kind of conversation where growth may be noted.

Couple and Family Therapy

Posttraumatic growth emerges in couple and family therapy as well. For example, couples that are dealing with the trauma of extramarital affairs sometimes remark that the affair acted as a catalyst for doing something about a troubled marriage. We have seen couples that have stated that they are glad that the affair occurred because it forced confrontation with their problems and set in motion concerted efforts to improve things. These affairs are truly traumatic in shattering assumptions about fidelity, commitment, and safety. They tend to break marriages as a result or initiate a process of reconstruction of a better form of relating.

In couple or family therapy, growth is often described by one family member who has noticed it in another. However, such growth has been recognized by family therapists as potentially threatening as well, upsetting a balance of power or roles in the family as one member becomes healthier, stronger, or able to shift perspective. Growth for one member of a family does not necessarily translate into growth for other members or for the family as a whole. For example, a teenage girl was raped by her stepfather, and as a result, she went to live with her biological father and his wife, with whom she had had relatively little contact. Her relationship with her father became much closer as she found herself turning to him for safety and reassurance. The daughter came to value this relationship highly and felt that her struggle with the aftermath of sexual assault had produced an important bonding with her father.

Another example of the challenge of posttraumatic growth is a couple who experienced the death of their child. The husband had had a drinking problem for years that the wife had tolerated. After the child's death, she told him, "Life is too short, I'm not putting up with your drinking any more. I won't expose our kids to it either. If I can deal with the loss of Karen, I can deal with losing you." In his grief, he seemed even less able or willing to get treatment and the wife ended up leaving him.

In working with couples and families who have experienced trauma, clinicians must be aware of the effects that posttraumatic growth may have on the functioning of relationships. Growth can challenge others in the family who seem to be left behind—unable to adapt to the changed ways of relating, priorities in life, or sense of strength and confidence of another family member.

FACILITATING POSTTRAUMATIC GROWTH AND MANAGED CARE

The impact of managed care in insurance coverage has changed the landscape of clinical practice. In the last 20 years, the number of psychotherapy clients whose mental health coverage is *managed* has increased dramatically and now dominates in most areas of the United States. A fundamental restriction that the managed care approach has introduced to the practice of psychotherapy is to limit the number of sessions that clinicians can have with particular clients. Another limitation is that the client's expenses in seeking professional help will be reimbursed only if the client has certain types of problems (typically only psychiatric disorders as defined by the current diagnostic manuals).

As any clinician now in practice knows, the typical managed care system doles out sessions in small chunks, some as few as one session. To qualify for reimbursement, subsequent sessions must be requested by the clinician, who must usually complete some sort of clinical update on client difficulties; the request must then be approved by a case manager at a central office. For persons with problems that require long-term therapy, this process must be repeated over and over again. At least in our experience, as the number of sessions the client has already had increases, the reluctance of the managed care system to grant additional sessions also increases. Therapists who request too many sessions for clients are likely to find themselves losing referrals from managed care systems.

For clients who come for help with difficulties precipitated by major life crises, it is possible that the current system may limit the possibilities for the exploration of posttraumatic growth through the limitation on the number of sessions that clients can have. Although we think this is unfortunate, it is the way things are currently. Even with the restrictions imposed by a system that rations psychotherapy sessions, however, we think it can be helpful for the clinician to approach clients struggling with the aftermath of trauma with a perspective that includes the possibility of posttraumatic growth.

Homework

The following chapters provide some specific examples of homework that clinicians may find helpful to employ with some of their clients and, in some instances, to use themselves. A main assumption that guides our current thinking about posttraumatic growth is that the process is initiated by the disruptive intrusion of the traumatic event. As discussed in chapter 1, traumatic events severely challenge or overwhelm the individual's worldview. This challenge is typically accompanied by high levels of psychological distress. It is in the process of rebuilding the new structure, the new set of assumptions that comprise the individual's worldview, that the greatest opportunity for posttraumatic growth exists. The sometimes radical transformations that characterize posttraumatic growth involve substantive changes in the variety of cognitive structures that individuals build to make their worlds predictable and meaningful.

One of the central uses of homework with clients dealing with crisis is to assist them to rebuild shattered assumptions (Janoff-Bulman, 1992). The process of schema rebuilding is not confined to homework. Much of what happens in clinical work with clients in the aftermath of highly stressful events is working with clients as they rebuild their worldviews. We have made an effort to offer homework that focuses on schema rebuilding that clinicians can choose to utilize with appropriate clients.

Some clinicians may be interested in assessing clients' beliefs and the degree to which posttraumatic growth has occurred. Following are two instruments that could be used with clients to make such assessments; they also serve as a springboard for further discussion in therapy.

The first instrument we have based loosely on the work of Janoff-Bulman (1989) and her World Assumptions Scale. Using a simple format like that suggested here may allow a client to consider what beliefs have withstood the trauma experience and which ones have been changed. Notice that the beliefs we have chosen focus on areas that survivors of trauma are often grappling with: the degree to which they have control over events, how benevolent the world and other people are, and whether there is a reason for things happening, and whether they are using their time in life in important and meaningful ways.

This is not meant to be an exhaustive list of basic beliefs or an accurate measure of them. This is simply a way for the therapist to help clients consider these issues. The clinician can then explore the implications of such changes for choices they are making and how the client may proceed through life.

Basic Beliefs

The following is a list of five categories of basic beliefs most people have some ideas about, although they may never examine them very carefully. Put a check mark next to what you thought before your crisis and a star next to what you think now. Some beliefs may have changed, some may be different. If what you believe is not among the choices, write your explanation.

Belief 1:

> *Really* bad things won't happen to me.
> Bad things are as likely to happen to me as anyone else.
> I was very worried that bad things would happen to me.
> I never really thought about this.
> I was confused about this.
> I had/have a different explanation.

Belief 2:

> I could manage most things, fix most things, and, as a result, most things would work out all right.
> Most things were beyond my control, but things would be all right in the end.
> I didn't think I could make things right, and most things would remain unresolved problems.
> I never really thought about this.
> I was confused about this.
> I had/have a different explanation.

Belief 3:

The world is generally pretty nice, and people will help me if I need it.

The world is a tough place, and there are a few people who will stick by you. You are lucky to be able to hang on to these few.

The world is a tough place, and I'd better not count on help from others.

I never really thought about this.

I was confused about this.

I had/have a different explanation.

Belief 4:

Things happen for a reason, and I was clear on what the reason is.

Things happen for a reason, but I wasn't clear on what the reason is.

Things just happen, not according to any particular reason or plan, but because of chance or people's decisions.

I never really thought about this.

I was confused about this.

I had/have a different explanation.

Belief 5:

What I'd been doing before the trauma with my time and energy is important and meaningful.

What I'd been doing before the trauma with my time and energy is not important and meaningful, but that didn't really matter to me.

What I'd been doing before the trauma with my time and energy is not important or meaningful, and that really bothered me.

I never really thought about this.

I was confused about this.

I had/have a different explanation

Belief 6 through?:

What other important beliefs did you have before your crisis, and now? List them here.

GROWTH

To determine where a client is in the process of growth, we offer a modification of the Posttraumatic Growth Inventory (PTGI), a 21-item instrument developed for research purposes to assess five domains of growth. The PTGI is reproduced in our book *Trauma and Transformation: Growing in the Aftermath of Suffering* (1995), and reliability and validity studies and normative data are available as well (see Tedeschi & Calhoun, 1996). The version herein includes a scoring system that may be more useful for clients and reduces items to 13. We do not recommend giving this to clients frequently, because something can be lost in reducing the growth experience for clients to a rating scale. However, it can be useful at some point for clients to consider specific growth themes and to prompt further reflection and discussion. The five domains of the original PTGI are represented: Appreciation of Life, New Possibilities, Spiritual Change, Relating to Others, and Personal Strength.

PTGI—Client Version

Consider the following statements in terms of how your struggle with trauma has initiated changes in you. Some of these things may represent ways you were before, therefore there may be little possible change in such areas. Look at these positive changes and rate them as follows: (a) "0" (This seems impossible for you to change), (b) "1" (You could imagine this happening for you, but you are not there yet), (c) "2" (You've had some thoughts about this yourself in the aftermath of this trauma), (d) "3" You've experienced this change to some extent following the trauma).

_____1. My priorities about what is important in life.

_____2. Trying to change things that need changing.

_____3. A feeling of self-reliance.

_____4. A better understanding of spiritual matters.

_____5. Knowing that I can count on people in times of trouble.

_____6. A willingness to express my emotions.

_____7. Being able to accept the way things work out.

_____8. Having compassion for others.

_____9. Seeing new opportunities that would not have been available otherwise.

_____10. Putting more effort into my relationships.
_____11. Developing a stronger religious faith.
_____12. Developing new interests.
_____13. Accepting needing others.

If you rated all these items as "0," you may not yet be at a place where growth is evident for you. However, if you rated at least three or four items as "1" or above and your level of current distress is not too high, you may be ready to consider how to take what you have experienced and begin the task of re-creating aspects of your self and your life. If you have some ratings of "2" or "3," you have already begun the process of posttraumatic growth and may be able to further this process.

Notice that the ratings of "1" involve some intellectual idea that change is possible. Real change and real growth involves a combination of this intellectual understanding and an emotional, deeply felt commitment to this view.

4

Helping Clients Develop
New Views of Vulnerability
and Strength

A view of oneself as strong and able to handle subsequent traumas is one of the growth outcomes that we have seen in trauma survivors. The fact that one has endured the traumatic event and the difficult, seemingly overwhelming aftermath can be taken as an indicator of strength. Survivorship is strength, but how the survivor feels during the process often seems like weakness. Still, survivorship is probably the most obvious aspect of strength that clients will see. There are other aspects, however, that are more subtle.

When people come to understand that they have benefitted from their struggle with trauma, they often recognize a paradox: that they have come to see themselves as both stronger and more vulnerable. A further paradox is that the vulnerability is part of their strength. This chapter explores this experience and indicates how therapists can help clients to recognize and appreciate it. It also emphasizes alternative concepts of strength, or subtle strength, that clients may not have previously considered.

To a great extent, the clinician's job is to encourage cognitive processing of the crisis—a mulling over of the changes that have occurred in the self—and introduce or highlight the perspective that growth and development can occur through the experience of vulnerability or weakness. Clinicians must also make themselves vulnerable to the terrible stories survivors of trauma must recount, thereby demonstrating the strength that is evident in allowing oneself to be vulnerable to the trauma story.

VULNERABILITY AFTER TRAUMA

It is easy to see how trauma would provoke feelings of vulnerability. Truly traumatic events tend to confront people with their limits—to their power and their life span. They may see the possibility of death more starkly and recognize that there is only so much they can do to ward off death or make various aspects of their lives turn out the way they prefer. Like being lost on a moonless night, persons enduring trauma are unsure of the path home, if they will ever reach it, or how much discomfort they will confront in getting there. This sense of vulnerability can lead to great anxiety or despair. So where does growth come in? It certainly does not come in the denial of this vulnerability and the feelings it engenders, but in confronting these existential issues about limited control over life and in sharing this experience with others.

One of the elements that make events traumatic is the undeniability that something terrible has actually happened. The situation is so clearly threatening that a person must face it or develop massive unhealthy symptoms of denial. This also is one of the elements that therapists should value in situations that clients face because such situations help provoke progress by shattering denial, resistance to change, old habits, and the like. Help then becomes necessary in the client's mind, and clients can be much more motivated after their old methods of operating are no longer functional. The old ways not only are unsuitable for the situation, but they become unsuitable for the changed person because after trauma the person is forever different. So the vulnerability that results from trauma is the therapist's ally, even if it does not appear to be an ally to the client initially. It destabilizes dynamic balances of a person's life—intrapersonal or interpersonal—that ordinarily accommodate or absorb change (Baumeister, 1994; Watzlawick, Weakland, & Fisch, 1974), forcing new adaptations.

FINDING THE STRENGTH

Trauma Expertise As a Strength

It appears that this exploration of the trauma and the aftermath transforms clients into trauma experts. They get to know the trauma inside and out. By being vulnerable to it, they do the most complete exploration. Eventually this thorough knowledge obtained through vulnerability becomes a source of great strength. They come to know the details and nuances of trauma; in the process, aspects of themselves that never would have been uncovered otherwise are considered. Traumas that involve physical endurance, war, captivity, disaster, and the like make clear that physical and psychological resources are tapped into by survivors that they appreciate for a lifetime. However, trauma that may be predominantly psychological, like the death of a loved one, also has the same sense of endurance about it. In either case, the endurance is as much a psychological battle as a physical one, and this is the strength that tends to be recognized most clearly—the psychological strength to simply go on (e.g., blind faith and determination in the face of the tunnel that seems so long that no light comes from the other end).

Some clients who endure trauma have never thought of themselves as particularly strong. They have much to gain in their endurance. Because they may have been the kind to shrink from challenges and difficulties, this trauma forced on them provides an opportunity to grow that they would never have otherwise had. Simply the recognition that "I can't believe I'm still alive through this!" can change self-concept from weakling to a person of strength. A study of people with a variety of orthopedic disabilities found that half felt that the disability had provided certain advantages—most often the opportunity to test themselves against a challenge. One person said, "It has allowed me the opportunity to overcome something which, before it happened, I would have not believed I could overcome" (Weinberg & Williams, 1978, p. 32). However, survivors of trauma may protest, "I've merely survived, doggedly and without any plan." However, such survival is worthy of respect, especially this kind of survival, where one has been functioning purely on instinct. The person surviving in this way may come to have greater respect for his or her own instincts and be able to trust them and act on them. For example, grieving people who cannot follow the instructions of others to *move on* may find that their own way of grieving actually works, eventually leading them into a life that they can live. The therapist's job is to support the instinctual moves of the client, helping clients see what is right about their own perceptions and choices and how much they can count on these strengths. The client may end up being much more assertive and self-confident in the end.

Strength Before and After Trauma

Experiencing vulnerability may be most difficult for a person whose identity before the trauma involved a sense of invulnerability or great strength. In this case, identity is most clearly altered, and the client who is like this may desperately want to return to the former self. To address this, it is useful to consider the self as composed of a number of elements of identity. Generally, people manage trauma better when they can recognize that there are different aspects to their identity and when one seems weak or threatened, another remains intact (Showers & Ryff, 1996).

> *Therapist*: When do you find yourself still being strong, like some part of that old you? Is that old you ever still apparent to you?
>
> *Client*: Yes, but sometimes I think I just can't go on living like this!

The therapist can help the client identify moments of peace or at least how the client is still standing after being hit by waves of emotion. The therapist might point out the strength in the attempt to survive.

> *Therapist*: But you are still living through it. You are here with me, trying to figure it out. That takes some strength. It takes a lot of strength to continue when you are feeling so weak.

Hence, the client is confronted with the paradox of vulnerability and strength again—that people get stronger by confronting weakness.

Of course, therapy involves the use of conversation to accomplish all these things. However, at some point, persons who are coping with the aftermath of trauma may begin to feel like they should not have to talk about this anymore. One client who had gone through terrible chemotherapy and stem cell treatment for cancer said afterward that she felt like a complainer when telling her husband about her difficulties. Although her husband was very supportive and showed no indication that he was tired of this talk, she felt guilty about it. The clinician made a deal that she could talk all she wanted, but would not *whine* to him. Just by introducing another word, *whine*, she had something she could avoid while all the rest of the talk became all right with her. She got to show her weakness in this relationship, but not so much that she felt weak.

Subtle Strength

Part of the problem that trauma survivors have in finding strength rests with their old definitions of strength. Men in particular may have difficulty with this because their definitions tend to have a lot to do with conquering or fixing things, doing much of this independently, and not expressing any weaknesses. However, vulnerability appears as an apparent contradiction to this viewpoint, implying emotional expressiveness and support seeking. In the aftermath of trauma, many people feel like weaklings or failures because they were not able to prevent the trauma, they are not able to reverse it, their emotions can overwhelm their ability to manage, and they do not know how to proceed. Thus, the therapist must introduce the idea of subtle strength. This is the strength of endurance, acceptance, expressiveness, and support seeking—tendencies that may have previously been viewed as vulnerability. Clinicians familiar with constructivist approaches may see clearly how this may demand fundamental shifts in schemas that are used to define identity. Survivors who have defined themselves as strong in particular ways will need to redefine strength. Those who have considered themselves to be vulnerable must notice that survivor status must connote strength. That is not to say that survivors should be encouraged to reconstrue everything as strength. Vulnerability is real, and trauma tends to verify that. Instead, an existential truth is reckoned with. A clear-eyed acknowledgment of vulnerability demands the courage to live in the face of death.

The juxtaposition of vulnerability and strength can be seen clearly in support groups for persons surviving particular crises. In the disclosure that happens in the group, people make themselves interpersonally vulnerable. This appears to be the case for men in particular, who seldom have the experience of *breaking down* in tears before others—men, women, or strangers. It is a huge risk that is often taken unwillingly. The tears may come simply because they cannot be held back in the telling of their experience. Inevitably there is acceptance of this by the group, and this can be a revelation to the man who cried. To be in a relationship with others and emotional like this may be an experience that many men have rarely had. Of course, the people that they are vulnerable to in these groups are other trauma survivors too. This is a select, specific group of persons to reveal oneself to. Nevertheless, emotional self-disclosure is still risky and uncomfortable, and probably never would have happened if the trauma had not reduced the man's ability to manage emotional distress. The inability to have control of oneself in this situation allows for all kinds of possibilities: deep intimacy and the experience of acceptance when the social veneer is stripped away. Without needing to be preoccupied with maintaining decorum, such a client may be free to be much more expressive than usual, allowing him to discover aspects of self and ways of relating that had not been previously explored. This person also becomes safe for others to disclose to, allowing for more experiences of interpersonal intimacy. The next chapter discusses more of these relationship developments. The point here is that being able to relate to others in this freer, more expressive way is ultimately experienced as a strength—the strength of being vulnerable, without worrying much about it.

These developments involve redefining strength. Old versions of strength did not protect against the horror of the trauma or promote recovery from it. However, feelings of vulnerability and distress make it difficult for clients to see themselves as strong. With emotions unexpectedly arising and an acute sense of loss, it is hard to experience oneself as strong. However, to be emotionally healthy, all of us have to have some sense of strength. So the therapist must help the client redefine strength to include what previously seemed weak. Some clients can grasp this essentially on their own. One man who was a top salesman for a textiles firm reflected on the changes in him since his wife left him. He had been utterly preoccupied with making money in his early adult years so that later he and his family would have the *good life* and enjoy themselves. In the process, he was brusque, demanding, self-centered, and physically and emotionally unavailable to his wife and children. After he found there was nothing he could do to get his wife back, despite attempts to be more attentive to her, he decided that his new way of relating was actually good for him, and he felt calm and strong in taking time out for people rather than being driven. His old way of being looked like the way of a man on the run, frightened of failure, and desperate for security. He never had seen himself in this light previously. What used to look like strength was now viewed as a kind of vulnerability. What used to look like vulnerability was now seen as strength.

One of the themes that therapists can keep in mind as they help clients redefine strength in the aftermath of trauma is that facing fear is strength. Because trauma brings people face to face with issues in living that are usually avoided; the client has come face to face with what has been feared. This is not of their own volition, some clients argue, so it does not count. However, the client still has choices in how to face it.

Client: But it doesn't seem like I have any choice. These feelings just come over me and I can't keep them away.

Therapist: Well, some people put up a big fight to keep them away. They drink. They immerse themselves in activity. You aren't, so to me you are making a choice to do the difficult thing.

Client: It still doesn't feel like any choice to me.

Therapist: Well, you are here talking to me about it—that is facing it, too.

Client: Only because I thought I'd die if I didn't talk to someone.

Therapist: So you are talking about something that makes you feel helpless, admitting and facing what you see as weakness. A lot of people just can't do it. Although this may not seem like an act of strength to you now, and we could debate this one for a long time, it may be that at some point you'll see the outcome of facing this as strengthening you—in ways you haven't thought of as strength before.

The therapist looks forward to possibilities and foreshadows ways of thinking for the client. Even if the client cannot quite grasp it yet, a therapist who reaches a little into the hopeful future of the client—but not too far—introduces a new schema at some embryonic level. Clients often rediscover this later as their own construction, although the clinician may make a tentative reframing of the client's idea of weakness. We have discussed this elsewhere in the use of labels of *survivor* versus *victim* to promote the sense of strength that can be apparent when people live through trauma, have the good sense to seek support, and posses the courage to disclose their distress (Tedeschi, Park, & Calhoun, 1998). As Lance Armstrong, a former top-ranked cyclist who was struck by cancer, has said, "Now, I'm better known as a cancer survivor. I just love that word—survivor" (Becker, 1998).

Of course, as mentioned in chapter 3, therapists must take care not to get too far ahead of the client. If they do, they would lose credibility by suggesting pat answers or by suggesting some hopeful future without having understood the complete picture of the client's distress. Such introductions of new ways of thinking about strength can only come on the basis of close listening and being emotionally touched by the client's situation. We believe that posttraumatic therapy cannot be effective, nor can it encourage growth most successfully, without the emotional availability of the therapist to the horror of the trauma.

All of this is predicated on the assumption that the client is far enough past the occurrence of the trauma to have left behind the numb feeling, and has gotten far enough along in the process of healing, either through therapy or without it, that he or she is emotionally open. For some clients, this may happen quite early on. However, clients who cannot yet allow themselves to be emotionally vulnerable, who are not in a successful defensive posture, are probably not ready to move along the path of posttraumatic growth. Furthermore, survivors of trauma must have at least short periods of respite from emotional turmoil to reflect on their experience and process it into new schemas that will be experienced as transformation of their lives. Again, vulnerability is the ally as long as the effect that heightens the sense of vulnerability is not constant. At first there is only a wish to somehow get through what has happened, with no sense that benefits could be possible. That is too high a goal to contemplate and should not be suggested by a clinician early on in therapy.

Metaphors of Survival and Growth

Metaphors can act as powerful messages to promote schema change or new worldviews (Kopp, 1995; Siegelman, 1993) in the course of psychotherapy. Certain metaphors are particularly apt in the case of trauma survivors, describing the experience of loss, emotional distress, and uncertainty about the future. Clients may experience their emotional life like a series of waves that wash over them and then recede. They may also think of themselves as crossing a burning, empty desert, but miraculously find oases every so often. The therapist can talk with clients within these metaphors—How high are the waves? How often do they come? Do they leave you standing or do they knock you down? Can you find your footing again? Do you feel refreshed at all or just pounded? Do you feel in any danger of being washed out to sea? Answers to such questions allow survivors to see how vulnerable they are and how much strength they have in the face of these elements.

The therapist can return to these metaphors to help clients see progress over time. In contrast to sterile abstractions, such as rating scales of distress, these images often carry more affective weight and give the client a better sense that the clinician understands the posttrauma experience. Also, the vulnerability and strength of the client are more evident in such metaphorical images. For example, think of the client as struggling across the desert to the oasis. At first there is nothing but hot sand in all directions and no sense of direction. The client walks on nevertheless, on blind faith and determination to survive. On finding the surprising oasis, the client may gain hope that another will be found. The client might discover a camel to ride—who is this friend? The development of hope, confidence, and eventually a way out of the desert become possible. Working with images introduces the possibility within the metaphorical environment first. Then it is translated into the life possibility of the client. The client might first start to think, is there a way out of this desert? Later the client might recognize that this question about the way out of the desert is also a consideration that there might be a way out of suffering. To find it would require much courage, cleverness, and determination (and perhaps some help from their camel or a guide). However, their strength in persevering is certainly a necessity.

Clients who are not far enough along in the posttrauma experience may not be able to relate to any metaphor of a journey. Instead, they might feel like they are on a ride they have never been on before—like a roller coaster someone stuck them on against their will. This is no journey, but a kidnapping. It is harder to see one's strength in such a situation. Instead, the status of passive victim is more evident and the vulnerability is abundantly clear. From this position, where and how does growth develop? First, the forced ride on the roller coaster may be the greatest challenge of the person's life. It is important to maintain this challenge perspective even if it is an unwanted challenge. Second, staying within the framework of this particular metaphor, the client must come to recognize that they are making choices while they are kidnapped. The therapist might talk with the client about this aftermath of trauma as additional torture, beyond the event itself. Even victims of torture make choices about how much to resist their captors. They may be learning self-comforting or dissociative techniques. The clinician can reframe these as clever and fundamentally human ways of coping rather than indications of pathology. Regardless of whether clients conceive of themselves as strong, weak, or neither, one common experience is often this concern about how *normal* their posttrauma experience is. By asking the client about certain experiences, the therapist indicates that he or she knows that these are likely and have been described by others.

A mother of a murdered child described what it was like for her to come to therapy. She looked forward to it until the time came and then she would get acutely anxious. Yet she did come to face the painful feelings in the aftermath of her daughter's death. She made a choice to come despite the pain, and this was an act of courage, although it also had the feeling of necessity. It was difficult for the client to see things this way for a while. The therapist must note the courage and strength while not discounting the pain and effort involved. These are no easy choices. The therapist can help the client locate the elements of choice, courage, and strength in the midst of the pain, fear, and vulnerability, and metaphors can sometimes make these elements more distinct.

On the roller coaster, certain choices remain possible— to scream or not? To breathe or hold your breath? To look around or close your eyes? These are the choices the trauma survivor has made and may continue to make during their period of being kidnapped. Metaphors can be particularly helpful while discussing this potential growth experience, because most trauma survivors have never experienced anything quite so difficult before. They do not have the words to explain it exactly and the metaphors help. It is important that the clinician collaborate with the client on the metaphor to make sure that it suits. For example, we have seen that for some clients, the *journey* is a useful metaphor, because they see themselves as active, moving forward, and having some strength. Others who feel more passive and still victimized may find the roller coaster more descriptive. Consider how these metaphors can be adapted. On the journey, one could be kidnapped, thus it becomes a forced march. Others' expectations for recovery are like a poke in the back from the captors. What role does the therapist play? Is the therapist always alongside, or does he pop out of the bushes on occasion to accompany the client only to disappear again?

It is especially effective when clients offer their own metaphors, but some are more likely to do this than others. At the least, clinicians can offer metaphors that are within the client's frame of reference or life experience so that the surplus meaning of the metaphor is readily available to the survivor.

Therapist: You told me you like to play basketball, as I remember.

Client: Yeah, that's right.

Therapist: I was thinking about how you feel you should be strong enough to deal with this on your own, and it reminded me of basketball.

Client: What do you mean?

Therapist: You know how sometimes there is a player on the other team that is just so much bigger, or so much quicker, it is hard to find anyone to guard him?

Client: Sure.

Therapist: You know what you might have to do, don't you?

Client: Double-team him?

Therapist: Yeah, that's what I was thinking.

Client: So?

Therapist: I think you're up against something so big, we've got to double-team it—you and me together.

Client: One of those situations where a plain-vanilla defense won't do.

The way the metaphor is offered can have a great impact. The metaphor about the strength available in support, and how there is no shame in changing defenses in extraordinary situations, could have been presented all at once, with the therapist giving it all to the client. However, the therapist teases the client to get his attention—to get him involved in where he is going with the metaphor. Of course, by doing it this way, the therapist puts the double-team into practice, rather than going off on his own.

Metaphors offered by a client can reveal much about how the client experiences things now and what is possible in the future. Some clients who describe a very difficult time posttrauma, and who appear to be having a great deal of difficulty managing, can sometimes offer metaphors that hint at strength and change that they cannot yet perceive in their more prosaic descriptions of their situation. One client had seen the movie "Titanic" and talked about the horror of those who died and those who survived. The discussion turned to how the survivors had lost forever their innocence and other valuable aspects of themselves. The clinician, who had fortunately seen the movie as well, remarked on a scene at the beginning of the film. An object recently recovered from a safe removed from the ship's wreck on the ocean floor is processed on the salvage vessel. The slim rectangular object is placed in a small protective tank, unrecognizable because it is covered with a heavy layer of silt deposited over the years. A worker begins to clean away the silt with a small hose. At first it is unclear what the objects is. As the small hose slowly does its work, the head, then neck and then the torso of a beautiful young woman emerge from the gunk. In a scene shortly after, the director of the expedition accepts a phone call from an elderly woman who asserts that she knows something about a valuable necklace that disappeared in the wreck. The director asks, "Can you tell us who the woman in the picture is?" "Oh yes," the woman replies. "The woman in the picture is me." This became a way for the client and therapist to talk about recovery of the self, the possible rediscovery of one's true self that may have been covered up over the years, and what survives trauma.

A bereaved mother who was a paramedic was a first responder at the scene of her son's automobile accident. She had been unable to return to work, and had become virtually homebound, afraid to venture out onto the roads in fear of coming across an accident scene. She offered the following description of her work in her garden: "I get down into the dirt and dig, pull up the weeds, and ideas come to me about what to plant where, and how to make this really beautiful. Then these plants start to grow, and it surprises me that all that beauty has come out of this weed-infested spot I never paid attention to before." Now this client was simply describing how she had been gardening at home because she could not do much else at this point. However, there are obvious expressions of hope, change, and growth in this that can be mined judiciously by a therapist. For example, the clinician at this point, or at a later date, might first make a connection between the present and the weed-infested plot: "Things for you remind me a bit of that weed-infested plot that was the site of your garden." Then see if the client makes the link—between the hard work and the therapy or grief process—or the next link—between the beautiful garden and the future. If not, let it be, and perhaps a bit later on the other links can be approached again.

THE CLINICIAN'S WAY OF BEING: VULNERABLE
AND INVULNERABLE

Vulnerability produces changes in identity, patterns of relating, the sense of control people have over their lives, and how meaningful their lives are. In the midst of crisis, most people feel like they are falling apart because indeed the old ways of operating have fallen apart in the seismic events. A good clinician does not avoid these events, although they may be horrible for the client, and likely would be horrible for the therapist to experience as well (see chap. 7).

In fact, a trauma therapist may sometimes have to convince clients to tell their whole story, sparing no detail, or the therapist will find it harder to feel enough of the emotional impact of the trauma to be effective in the work with the client. Clinicians may need to show the client that they are willing to confront the horror. The therapist might have to say, "I know this might be hard for you to recount, but I need to hear all that you can bear to tell me. I really need to understand as much as possible what this was like in order to be most helpful for you. So when you are ready, please tell me as much as you can. And of course, we can do this in bits and pieces if you'd like." This can be a powerful invitation—an indication that the therapist is ready to withstand the onslaught of grief, fear, anger, and other strong emotions and unpleasant details. The therapist is telling the client not to hold back—that he or she can take it. Then, of course, the clinician must be ready. It is important for the therapist to realize that the client may not wish to recount the trauma. Thus, while the invitation is issued, it is made clear that the client can choose what parts to tell and when to do it. We have encountered some clients who fled therapy because clinicians were demanding a detailed recounting while the clients were trying to manage things by distancing themselves from the events. Again it is important to realize that the work we are describing is generally with trauma survivors who have already moved through the immediate shock of events and perhaps some initial trauma therapy to help them with distress.

Instead of becoming overwhelmed, a clinician can show vulnerability to the affect of the client; he or she can be touched by the client's experiences while maintaining an ability to cope with the client's distress and remain hopeful about the future. This hopefulness exists even as the therapist is uncertain about the client's future. However, the clinician needs a firm sense of faith in the client's ability as a human being to somehow manage this trauma. In doing this, a client can experience vulnerability and strength in another person perhaps before seeing how these might coexist in the self.

Clients who are experiencing the aftermath of trauma may wonder how clinicians deal with trauma clients and if they have any hope.

Client: How can you sit there all day and listen to stuff like this? Doesn't it drive you crazy? Doesn't it get you down?

Therapist: I have hope. I have seen others get through these things, and I believe that the therapy will be useful in this regard. So I can listen while I imagine that you will feel better about things someday.

Of course, this hopefulness is only convincing if it is real. That is why this kind of clinical work is especially tough for beginning therapists who have not yet seen enough hopeful outcomes or experienced the power of effective therapy in producing them. The hopefulness can only be perceived by clients to be real if the therapist has listened closely and openly enough so that the client senses that the therapist has been touched by the trauma—has felt it. If the therapist, knowing the depth of the pain, fear, or loss, can be hopeful, this hopefulness is not easily dismissed. However, the therapist who has not listened openly enough to be touched does not have this credibility because he or she has not shared in the vulnerability.

In sharing the vulnerability, therapists cannot experience the same intensity as their clients. First, if they do, they will discount the client's experience—it is the client's trauma and emotion so no one else can or should feel it as acutely. Second, the client is reassured when he or she has someone who can act as a container for these emotions—someone who can gather them up and keep them until the next session and demonstrate the strength of being able to withstand them. A therapist who is open and vulnerable to the trauma is seen as strong because this is a person who has not shied away from the powerful emotion that the client feels.

Symptom Control as Counterproductive?

There can be a disadvantage in excessively brief, symptom controlling therapy for trauma. If the trauma and disorganization it promotes are viewed as potential allies in the movement toward positive change, the therapist should not be in the business of short-circuiting this process. The psychological disruption produced by trauma makes growth possible. A clinical strategy that focuses exclusively on emotional control may inadvertently give the client the impression that the therapist is threatened by all this and is not strong enough to help.

Many other people in the client's life may be reacting this way—wanting all these emotions to stop and for the client to calm down. They are frightened and inconvenienced by all this *trauma stuff* and want the original person back. When clients describe these reactions in others, it can be helpful to address what the client already knows—that it is unimaginable that they will be able to be the way they used to be. This is reassuring because the client knows this too. Then the question is, who is this new me and how will I relate to these people? Questions of identity and relating have to be sorted out.

> *Therapist*: That's too bad for your friends and family, because you are different now, they can't have the old you back.
>
> *Client*: Well, this new me is good for nothing.
>
> *Therapist*: The new you is a work in progress, and it is hard to know exactly how to relate while you are under construction. But we seem to relate OK, and I like what I see.

Again, such statements indicate the hopeful comfort the therapist has with this process and the trust the therapist has in the client's ability to get through it. Of course, it is easier for the therapist to be patient with all this—he or she is not experiencing the clients distress.

> *Client*: But I don't know how long I can go on feeling this way. You don't have to live like this every day. You don't have to feel these things that just get overwhelming!
>
> *Therapist*: Of course, you are right. But that allows me to provide a safe haven for you when you are most upset.An emphasis here is on the steadfast strength of the therapist through all of this while allowing for the truth that the client's distress is understandably more intense. The therapist operating in this way can be thought of as an emotional *container*. However, the therapist must not contain or limit so much that the message is given that the client's emotions and experiences are dangerous and not to be trusted.

Homework

Homework assignments can be useful in helping the client notice strength and positive change that can be easily glossed over or misunderstood. The previous chapter offered some simple paper-and pencil-exercises to help clients notice changes in their beliefs and tendencies toward growth. However, for many trauma survivors, homework must be simple and straightforward enough to avoid introducing additional burdens or failure experiences, and even simple exercises may be too much for some.While respecting what the client is capable of, we tend to suggest that the client do some basic self-monitoring that introduces the concept of strength during a period of vulnerability. It is often best to design specifics of assignments collaboratively with each client so that his or her expertise in the trauma recovery is respected.This chapter focused on helping trauma survivors notice their strength in times of vulnerability and how even vulnerability can be a kind of strength. An obvious assignment would be to have a client monitor and record when they experience themselves as strong. A more challenging exercise is the following. Ask clients to identify perceived weaknesses and look for strength in those instances. Following is an example of how this assignment might be made.

Therapist: We've been talking about how it has been hard to notice any ways you are strong through all this—that you think of yourself as a weakling. I think it would be good for you to pay closer attention to the strength. Each day, take an experience that you view as a failure, and ask yourself, "In what way did I show some strength in that situation?"

Client: I think that will be hard to see.

Therapist: Let's try it together and see. What happened this week that seemed like a failure on your part?

Client: Well, I couldn't go to the store wearing this wig (to cover hair loss from chemotherapy). I was too embarrassed.

Therapist: When did you get the wig?

Client: Before I started chemo. I figured I might need it. But now I'm not using it!

Therapist: How did you think the wig would help?

Client: Well, I figured it would make it easier to go out.

Therapist: So, in this case your strength was wanting to continue to go out and stay active while undergoing the chemotherapy, and looking for some way for that to be possible.

Client: Yeah, but I felt funny going out in it.

Therapist: But it was an attempt to address this problem. Trying ways to solve a problem looks like a strength to me, even if not every solution is immediately successful.

Client: I see what you are saying, but it is hard for me to look at things that way.

Therapist: Right. That's why I was thinking this might be a good exercise for you. You could practice this way of seeing yourself. I'll bet you'll be able to see strengths sometimes, other times not. And if it is hard to notice the strength in a particular situation you've been dealing with, bring it back here next time and we'll look at it together.

Notice how the way of presenting such an assignment demonstrates the therapist's hopeful approach and trust in the client. The therapist acknowledges that the client will not, and does not, have to be successful in every attempt to notice a strength. However, by giving the assignment, the clinician is saying that she believes the strengths are there. The assignment also introduces the idea of subtle strength.Here is another possibility for an assignment on vulnerability and strength.

Therapist: You've been saying that you have no idea how to be strong in situations like this.

Client: Right, I just don't know how people get through this! I know they do, but I just can't imagine.

Therapist: I'd like you to try to think of people you think of as strong, and imagine what they would do if they had to go through what you are. Imagine them in your spot—what would their way be?

Client: You don't mean just someone who has been through this, but anyone?

Therapist: Anyone you think of as strong—someone you know personally, someone you've read about or been told about. Anyone you want to use that you think of as strong, what do you think they would do? You might try this with more than one person, and just write down some of the things you imagine they'd do to cope.

This assignment gets people thinking about coping abilities that they do not identify with themselves; it can act as a springboard to some attempts to define what strength in their situation would look like. Sometimes clients come back without any ideas of what anyone would do—that others who are strong would be as devastated as they are. This is also useful. Then the clinician can say, "So even the strongest people you can think of would be at a loss to handle something like this." The clients are no longer especially vulnerable, but normally, humanly vulnerable.

5

Helping Clients Make Changes in Relationships

Helping clients make changes in how they relate to others is a common goal of the psychotherapy enterprise. This chapter examines how clinical work with persons who have experienced traumatic events can aid in that work. This will build on the material from the last chapter, where we saw how clients may reconsider their self-schemas, seeing themselves as both stronger and more tender. This paradoxical sense of self may be the best vantage point from which to see new possibilities in relating. The way a survivor relates to others after a trauma is built on the interpersonal patterns established before the trauma, together with the reconsideration of self noticed as a result of the schema changes initiated by the trauma. Some clients might experience the trauma as a greater change than others.

Our clients often enter therapy because of a precipitating event; a truly traumatic experience cannot only precipitate symptoms, but it can also create an openness to change. Therapy must offer an atmosphere of psychological and physical safety for the symptoms of posttraumatic stress to be addressed, and this same safe atmosphere can also encourage the exploration of further change in the direction of posttraumatic growth. Let us consider how growth can be reflected in the client's interpersonal relationships and then talk about how to encourage this process through the therapy relationship.

POSTTRAUMATIC GROWTH IN RELATIONSHIPS

Certain changes in relating are possible after surviving a trauma. Survivors of trauma may find people of value, worth relating to, when they

91

had not before. Survivors may change the way they engage in these relationships, how they present themselves, or the role they take with other people. Survivors may also experience an increased closeness in their relationships with significant others.

Finding New Value and Greater Closeness in Relationships

Positive posttraumatic changes in relating tend to involve a recognition that one cannot go it alone in life, and there come times when interdependence with others becomes clear. Weakness and vulnerability must be admitted to others, opening up the possibility that they might help in a way that has never been necessary or experienced before. Consider the experience of Wayne Ross, a young man who was on a 16,000-mile bicycle ride from Alaska to Argentina to raise money for multiple sclerosis when an accident with a bus paralyzed him. Interviewed a year later by Leslie Kussmann, a film producer, he said:

> I went from being extremely independent to extremely dependent on everyone and everything. I am now dependent on assisted devices, lift vehicles, home healthcare, family and friends. My view of the accident is everything happens for a reason. In trying to set a new record in biking, I broke my neck. The positive thing that has come from my injury is a better relationship with my family and friends. … My mom has surprised me time and time again with her boundless energy and positive attitude. My father and I have had a chance to reconnect in ways that might never have happened otherwise. … When I was in the hospital in Boston, many of my old high school and college friends came to visit me. I was shocked. Some of these people I hadn't seen in years. It meant a lot to me that my old friends still cared and remembered me. … This accident has caused me to take a 180 degree turn around. It has forced me to change my ways. I have realized the importance of interpersonal skills … . (Kussmann, 1997–1998, p. 37)

Often the people who are seen as needed and most helpful are others that have endured similar experiences. As clinicians, we have often heard bereaved persons say, "You have been very helpful, and so nice to talk to, but I really need to be with other people who have gone through this." Part of the reason is that the survivor of trauma wants to be assured that it is possible to continue to have a life after this event. Are other survivors normal people, having some kind of satisfying life? They are also looking for models of how to carry this off. If another has done this, perhaps they can too and also discover how this may be accomplished.

Another value in being with other survivors is the sense of acceptance—that others understand in a way that those who have not gone through this cannot. The long-standing bonds evident in war veterans' organizations attest to this, as does the fact that veterans tend to group according to which war they were in. People generally want company at least at some points in the aftermath of their trauma, as long as the company is someone who is seen as really being able to understand. Otherwise they would rather be left alone. One woman whose teenage son was murdered withdrew from her work and social connections completely in the first few months after her son's death. However, she looked forward daily to visits from her son's friends who would spend time talking to her about her son, their memories of him, and their grief. Once they started to move on to other topics and leave her son out of the discussions, their presence was not so valued anymore. The bond created by the experience of similar traumatic experiences often transcends all kinds of boundaries of economic status, education, and other life experiences. A trauma survivor's circle of relationships may be broadened in this way.

Another specific manifestation of posttraumatic growth is the way in which experiencing the struggle with trauma is a gift: an increased compassion for and ability to empathize with other hurting people, particularly those who have suffered similar crises. This can be the basis for closer emotional relating than was possible before. Survivors also learn what has been helpful to them, what to do and what not to do for others. Therefore, they may relate differently to others than they have in the past.

Benny W.: Trauma As Tenderizer

Benny was a 42-year-old man who had suffered the loss of his 10-year-old daughter after a 2-year battle with leukemia. He came to therapy in desperate grief, unable to work, and feeling isolated from the world, which had continued seemingly unaffected by his daughter's death.

Benny never would have imagined himself in therapy before all this happened. He considered himself to be capable and unsentimental. He was surprised at the emotional toll his daughter's suffering and death had taken on him and was unable to relate to friends and coworkers in his old style: joking, kidding, making fun of weakness, and being generally uncomfortable with any serious discussion. His aggressive humor was his strategy to relate to others and to avoid closeness at the same time. He came to therapy initially "to support his wife," who was also having a terrible time and who was angry with him for not being sufficiently responsive to her grief. This actually frightened him because he thought that the wife he loved very much was thinking of leaving because he couldn't "be there for her."

Therapy initially focused on Benny's wife, Helen, pouring out her grief while Benny was encouraged to listen to all this pain. He had been successfully avoiding listening to his wife talk about her grief for some time and this was initially very uncomfortable for him. But out of love for her, he remained steadfast despite this discomfort. Finally, a session came when he erupted with the following: "Helen, you think you're the only one hurting? Don't you know what this did to me? Don't you know why I can't seem to do anything? Don't you think I want to work? I feel like a dead man!" Benny cried for several minutes, something his wife had never seen him do, except at their daughter's funeral. Benny was surprised by his wife's reaction. She was extremely touched by this. Her anger with him dropped away as she saw her grief reflected in her husband, whom she thought didn't experience pain in the same way.

After he cried for a little while, she said, "Benny, I never expected you not to have feelings like this. I know this has messed you up something awful. You just would never say anything about it, and you wouldn't listen to me. I'll listen to you all you want. That'll help me a lot, if you'd just talk to me. You can't joke your way through this, you know."

Traumas can change the dynamics of relating within couples, sometimes in highly positive ways. Just as trauma breaks up old ways of understanding one's own life, the changes wrought in individuals can allow partners to see aspects of the other person that they had never known before. Often this is useful in reconstituting schemas that have been used to predict the other's behavior and to determine what is possible in terms of relating. New possibilities for relating emerge. Helen found Benny to be more like her than she thought. Benny found Helen accepting and approving of what he thought to be an undesirable vulnerability. They came to consider that maybe they could be close in their grief rather than estranged. In sharing this emotional experience safely, there emerged the possibility that other difficulties could be brought into the light of day.

Maria S.: The Challenge of Breast Cancer

Maria is a 45-year-old broadcast journalist who is currently cancer free. She works for a radio station in a large metropolitan area. At the age of 35, a mammogram showed a small mass in her left breast. A biopsy revealed the growth to be malignant. She followed her physicians' advice and had a lumpectomy. Follow-up tests revealed no additional cancer.

Five years later, when she was 40, her annual physical revealed another mass, this time in her right breast. It was a recurrence of cancer. Immediately after the lump was identified, even before the biopsy results were back, she made an appointment for counseling. During her first session, she was noticeably, and understandably, upset. She reported that she was terrified, extremely worried, was having trouble thinking of anything else, and was "not ready to die yet."

She continued seeing the psychologist every few weeks or so for the next few months. This time she chose the option of a radical mastectomy, to be followed by a few weeks of chemotherapy. The psychologist worked primarily in a supportive role, listening and encouraging Maria's good coping strategies. Once again the cancer treatment was successful, although it was several months before she could allow herself to fully believe that the cancer had been eradicated.

During their final session together, the psychologist asked Maria what changes her struggle with the recurrence of cancer had made in her life. She described the many difficulties and side effects associated with the treatment, her terror over facing a potentially terminal disease, and her frequent worries about the recurrence of cancer. She also described how others had responded to her during the hard times. She put it this way:

> "I don't think I can accurately describe how the quality of some of my relationships has changed. It comes close to being that old cliche of 'words can not express,' you know? There's no doubt that some people I thought were my good friends turned out not to be. I guess they just couldn't take it this second time around. But going through this with Alvin [her husband] has made things ... deeper, closer. He's been there every step of the way. He didn't always know what to say to me, but he was always there. And he still is. It's like the proverb about still waters running deep. Well, our relationship now has a depth that I just can't describe. We are bonded in a way that just wasn't the case before *it* happened."

Maria's description is not uncommon in persons facing cancer, HIV infection, and other serious illnesses. It is a change in relationships that can include an experience of increased depth and closeness in relationships with others.

Posttraumatic positive changes in relating can happen in couples and family therapy, individual therapy (which of course still involves relating), and groups. Groups allow perhaps the greatest possibilities for changes in relating to others, especially when they are fairly homogeneous in terms of the type of crisis participants have faced. When a group of survivors share stories of their trauma and its aftermath, the universality of the experience is heightened and an atmosphere of safety supports possibilities for relating while the pain of trauma makes risks in relating necessary. These are primarily risks in the disclosure of affect.

Perhaps one of the best situations for posttraumatic growth in relating occurs when couples attend groups together. This may be the only arena where they feel free to deal with the trauma. At home they can be distracted by routine, cling to habits of relating, or feel that they need to be strong for the other, cutting off emotional expression. In groups spouses may see their partner relate to them and others in new ways. It is often hard not to be emotionally touched by someone else's trauma in such a situation, and partners who have difficulty talking about their own traumatic experience may be able to unite in discussing another's. Whatever the therapy setting—individual, couple, family, or group therapy—we can observe many of the same processes that promote new ways of relating to others.

Self-Disclosure of Vulnerability

The individual's experience with trauma usually has to come out. Some people simply have a compelling need to tell their story, whereas others make such disclosure only reluctantly. For persons who have resisted disclosure and intimacy in the past, the experience of telling about traumatic events and their aftermath can be an extension of the trauma experience. Their psychological survival may seem dependent on relating in this unfamiliar way, which is both uncomfortable and necessary. Disclosure offers opportunities for intimacy, as with Benny and Helen, described earlier.

Responses to the disclosure must be supportive, as Helen's was. She encouraged more talk and made it clear that she was accepting and willing to listen. There can be great subtlety in this. For example, in a bereaved parent group, one participant talked about how she felt responsible for her child's death. As soon as she began to mention this, another parent interrupted and stated strongly, "No! That's not right, you're not to blame." Although this comment may have been offered as support from one bereaved parent to another, its effect was to short-circuit this conversation. The opportunities for deeper relating opened up by self-disclosure are best responded to with invitations to hear more, appreciation for what has been shared, and not with quick-fixes, advice, or pat answers. This disclosure, particularly for survivors who are not used to it, is a delicate thing to be nurtured by the therapist. In group, family, or couple therapy, the therapist may have to intervene when someone else in the room is not responding in an inviting fashion to the disclosure. For example, in the case described, where one bereaved parent leapt to another's defense and declared they were not to blame, the therapist could say something like, "Although that might be apparent to us, I'd like to hear more about how you feel responsible."

Experiencing Support

After the disclosures about trauma and attempts to cope, the experience of support from the therapist and others in a family or group can be very comforting. Many persons are not used to receiving this comfort because they tend to do little disclosure. Exactly what is this *support* that the clinician needs to give? It is a nonjudgmental attitude—accepting the event, the survivor's reactions to it, and perspective. Given that in some cases trauma survivors see themselves as having contributed somehow to their own victimization by certain decisions they have made, it is important to be accepting rather than confronting. For example, one client who had been in an auto accident where passengers in a car he hit had died stated that if he had not been speeding and had been paying more attention to traffic conditions, the accident would not have happened. The clinician had to listen to his guilt and regret for several sessions before the client could begin to consider anything else. A striking change for this client was that before he had always had difficulty accepting responsibility or apologizing. Now it was necessary to relate differently to others, first with the therapist, to experience any relief. The client was now both accepting responsibility and making an implicit apology. The therapist's acceptance and support was a powerful interpersonal experience when this client felt so unworthy of it. The support is also a willingness by the therapist (and sometimes friends, others in a family, or group therapy setting) to go beyond the acceptance to being emotionally affected by the story of the trauma and aftermath. The most respectful response to such a story is to listen and be touched by it.

Listening to Others: Empathy Training
and Self-Awareness

When trauma survivors become listeners, (e.g., in family or group treatment), there are gains that become possible in how they relate to others. They may receive training in empathy as they try to understand the somewhat similar, somewhat different experiences and reactions of other survivors. A phenomenon often observed in trauma survivor groups is the recognition by group members that others have had it worse than they have. This downward social comparison (Wills, 1987) can be useful in relieving some distress, giving hope, and initiating a desire to help. Survivors come to recognize that they are not alone in their suffering, relieving them from trying to determine why they were singled out for this trauma (Taylor, Wayment, & Collins, 1993). This is expressed in such language as, "I thought my situation was bad, but I can't believe what she's going through!" Recognizing that one is not at the bottom of the barrel can allow people to see possibilities for themselves again. It is the outgrowth of listening well and being open to others' suffering. As group facilitators, we are often struck that these downward comparisons do not usually make logical sense. People who are making the comparison have often lived through worse circumstances than the persons to whom they compare themselves. It appears that the emotional openness of these specially equipped listeners allows them to respond more empathetically and sympathetically than nonsurvivors, which in turn allows them to use this comparative perspective. We have seen survivors tending to focus in their downward comparisons on specific aspects of the others' experiences, which they are thankful they did not have to face.

In addition to knowing others better, due to listening to the story of trauma, survivors may learn more about their own trauma and posttrauma experience from how someone else describes things. Others can put into words experiences that individuals have only dimly understood. The stories of others can become searchlights that peer into the dark corners of their own experience—places that they have been reluctant to look at themselves. In being empathic listeners, survivors sometimes find themselves considering things that have gone unexamined.

Support groups function according to the expectation that everyone can have an opportunity to tell their story and express themselves. This produces the expectation that others in the group will listen. Turning survivors who have to talk about their trauma into listeners who carry the perspective of trauma survival may provide a listening experience like none other. Survivors come to their compassion and fearless relating because the trauma has made listening to horrific stories necessary and healing, rather than something to be avoided, as it often might have been before. Again we see, as discussed in chapter 4, that vulnerability produces a subtle strengthening. Many trauma survivors become people who are more able to reach out to others in suffering and who are not afraid of emotion expressed by those who are reacting to trauma.

Lending Support: Giving to Others

The experience of lending support is often revealing for trauma survivors. This has been described well in the group therapy literature as one of the "curative factors" (Yalom, 1985). This experience can be encouraged by the therapist, but often survivors may feel compelled to share their *gift* of empathy. Others discover that they can lend support when they seek the support for themselves—when they want to be with other survivors to understand more about their own experience and what might be ahead of them. They might then encounter in their community, their own family, or in a support group persons who have been struck down by trauma as they have, for whom they have deep feelings of empathy and compassion, and whom they therefore attempt to help.

By helping others, survivors get outside their own situation and become oriented again to the world outside themselves. They may discover that they have something to offer—some residual strength. They also may discover that they realize something about the traumatic experience or its aftermath not seen by others or that they can stand to listen when others cannot.

Developing New Relationships

New relationships can come from the need to help others and to be with those who understand intuitively and experientially the survivor's position. These relationships may be temporary or may become a basis for an expanded social network. A sense of safety and community is fashioned from the aftermath of trauma through the development of such a network. What is often interesting about these networks is that, because they are based fundamentally on the shared experience of a certain kind of trauma, other personal characteristics that had once formed the basis for separateness and identity no longer count as much. In the fraternity of trauma survivorship, there is less attention paid to socioeconomic status, race, and the like. As a result, survivors may find themselves to be more accepting of people of other backgrounds because they have been able to bond with others on the basis of profound human experience, recognizing what is truly human about all of us.

Perhaps one of the most striking descriptions of the necessity of mutual support in the face of trauma comes from accounts of concentration camp experiences (Davidson, 1992). To survive in the camps, those interned often created small groups or little families based first on pairs as the basic unit, with structured rules that enhanced chances for survival. There was a need to help to have a purpose in survival, as well as a need to bond to survive. These intense bonding experiences not only allowed survival in the camps, but survivors used this capacity during their recovery and throughout life to develop strong support systems after the war. These survivors have seen themselves as psychologically stronger and more autonomous as a result of the struggle with these experiences.

A New Social Identity

Within the newness of relating with more vulnerability, affect, and disclosure comes the development of a different social identity. To a great extent, our sense of identity is formed in relation to other people, and therefore the new relating changes the sense of self; the responses of others to this new sense of self can bring on additional changes. These changes can be problematical in relationships with people who knew the survivor before the trauma. The *old self* seems to be gone, and friends and family may talk to the survivor about *being themselves* again. People who did not know the survivor before the trauma will not have to make such an adjustment in expectations. Survivors find that *being themselves again* is probably impossible. Their difficult experiences have changed them in fundamental ways and they cannot go back. Therapists can support this change and value the differences as well.

Some trauma survivors make rather conscious decisions to relate differently within the new approach to life that they are fashioning posttrauma (Frazier & Burnett, 1994). They may have a particular reason associated with their trauma experience to do so. For example, a rape survivor determined that she would never again allow herself to be dominated by a man, she would be more assertive, and she would respect herself more. She felt this was a way of making sure that the experience of rape was put to good use; she hoped that other women could use her as an example and therefore prevent themselves from getting into situations where they might suffer her fate. She created a new way of relating to both men and women that fostered her sense of strength.

A father whose young son died determined that he was going to relate differently to his two surviving sons. When he became frustrated with them, he would *speak* to his dead son in his mind, telling him that he would be patient with his surviving children. Chapter 3 described the father who was a little league coach who decided to change his coaching style after the death of his daughter. His new way was to recognize the specialness of every one of his young players, making sure they all had a chance to play, and that he was a supportive teacher to all of them. He did this consciously as a way to honor his daughter and put into action the love he recognized more clearly than ever in his grief. Many, if not most, times changes in relating come about without this kind of planning and may only be seen in retrospect. It can be useful for the clinician to point out such changes.

THE THERAPIST'S ROLE IN ENCOURAGING
NEW RELATIONSHIPS: SOME SPECIFICS

Connection with others who have experienced similar traumas is a healing experience for the vast majority of trauma survivors; it promotes new relationships as well as new ways of relating. These relationships and the ability to bond in a more profound, affective way represent some of the posttraumatic growth that we see in survivors. How does the therapist encourage this process?

Some survivors seem driven to find others with similar experiences, and therapists hardly have to do anything to encourage this process. Instead, therapists may need to become aware of community support groups and programs available or perhaps form support groups themselves. However, some survivors are reluctant to seek out others. This reluctance may be stronger in the early aftermath of trauma when emotions are still close to the surface. Men may be reluctant at this point because they do not wish to be seen as lacking control over themselves. This fear of losing control of one's emotional composure is common among survivors. In the early stages of recovery from trauma, when they are preoccupied by it and when it might define a new identity, survivors may feel compelled to *tell their story* in getting to know other people. Therefore, this step of networking may be most appropriate after survivors are able to talk about their trauma with enough composure not to embarrass themselves in front of a stranger. However, one of the most powerful experiences of a trauma survivor is to tell the story, including the strong emotion, and be welcomed and accepted by others. Making the telling too clinical and controlled can be counterproductive. Thus, clinicians might remember that clients are most ready for the development of new relationships when the story still has a good deal of affect available. For some survivors, the affect never goes away.

Therapists can help survivors decide what aspects of themselves they wish to reveal and what they decide they are not yet willing to share. This way the development of relationships has a degree of choice and control that is often reassuring. The therapist might also mention the aspects of the survivor's experience that are similar to what he or she has heard from other survivors, thereby emphasizing the availability of empathic responses. In doing so, the therapist also normalizes the survivor's experience so that the survivor can be less afraid of revealing certain things about him or herself. For example, one woman whose sister committed suicide was concerned about the feelings she had that her deceased sister had been manifesting herself at night. She had been reluctant to tell anyone about these experiences, and therefore had tended to avoid contact with potentially supportive people. After revealing this experience to the therapist and receiving reassurance that, although not universal, this was not unusual, it became easier for the client to be more open with others. The therapist, who was experienced in working with this population, also pointed out that the bereaved often yearn for some sign from the deceased and that her experience with the visitations would be highly valued by many. It is incumbent on therapists to know a good deal about the experiences of persons who survive the trauma their client is coping with to provide this kind of information, and therefore encourage self-disclosure and relationship development.

Sometimes therapists may role-play the beginnings of conversations that survivors can have with others as they begin to relate in unfamiliar ways. There will be people the survivor may want to disclose to, others they would like to avoid, and others with whom they prefer limited disclosure. The therapist can help the client decide who fits into each category. Some clients have not even thought that there could be such categories. Then the therapist and survivor can together develop responses that the survivor can use comfortably. Again these unfamiliar ways usually involve greater vulnerability and affect than previously, and this makes some clients quite uncomfortable at the beginning. However, these are the people for whom the posttraumatic experience can bring most gain.

Therapists can also bring to awareness the possibility that, because the trauma has changed the person, the person needs to consider what these changes are and how others will know about them. The experience of the trauma can be declared in how the survivor chooses to relate. The survivor then has the satisfaction of knowing, even if other people do not realize it, that "I am doing this in recognition of what I have been through, and who I am now." This way of interacting with others presents the survivor as a constructive rather than a damaged person.

The constructive use of survivorship can be made very public by some clients who transform their expertise in trauma into service to others and social action. Bloom (1998) pointed out how trauma survivors can educate their communities, serve as witnesses and seek justice, take political action, and express the trauma in artistic ways. In doing so, the survivor demonstrates strength, connects with others in ways that are mutually supportive, and creates some meaning out of the trauma. In the process, the survivor may benefit the society in ways that heal other survivors and prevent similar traumas in the future.

While encouraging these transformative activities, therapists need to be aware that, in some clients, such actions may short-circuit the process of examining and experiencing some personal, emotional aspects of the traumatic aftermath. Some clients might become wounded healers who are poorly equipped to help others constructively. As therapists, we try to alert clients to the challenges that certain activities might bring and help them understand their motives. For the vast majority of clients, however, we see the transformation of trauma into service as an extremely important sign of growth. This signals that the client has energy, hope, focus, and a recognition of personal strength and the gift of personal trauma experience. Social action can even help clients establish new identities and life paths.

A striking example of creativity and service in the aftermath of trauma is offered in a description of a Holocaust survivor whose trauma began when Nazis confiscated the bird collection he helped his father maintain. On liberation, he immigrated to Israel and began a bird collection that was open free to the public. Every child visitor would receive special attention from him in the form of a story about his father and his birds, the concentration camps, and his recovery in Israel. He saw his survival as intended to bring people closer to nature and to an understanding of the Holocaust (Davidson, 1992). This survivor was able to integrate his life before, during, and after the trauma, through this loving service.

Homework

The therapist can begin by asking clients to reflect on how the trauma has changed them. The therapist also can encourage survivors to consider what they would like others to understand about these changes or how they would like these changes to affect others. The client may then be ready to consider how to put the posttrauma changes into some kind of action. The client will have to try them out. When these are unfamiliar and uncomfortable, the self-talk that supports the decision to change and the determination that comes with having survived a trauma can be brought to mind to support the attempts to act in these new ways. Surviving the trauma is honored in these ways of relating to others, and the trauma becomes a useful part of the survivor's life. Suggesting some carefully chosen reading about their trauma, especially material written by other survivors, may be a good first step (see chap. 8).

6

Helping Clients Toward Philosophical and Spiritual Growth

Kathryn was a 22-year-old senior in college, her major was accounting, and she was engaged to be married. She had known her fiancée, Gerald, for 3 years and knew that they shared common interests in sports, movies, the theater, and music, and also that their fundamental values were the same. They both wanted careers, but they also planned to have children after they had been married for at least 2 or 3 years, and they wanted to share parental responsibilities. They also had a common commitment to the core beliefs and teachings of their independent, rather conservative, Protestant church. As Kathryn had once joked to one of her professors, quoting the words of a song popular at the time, the future that she and Gerald had was so positive and bright that "we have to wear shades."

In the spring semester of Kathryn's senior year, as they were returning from a weekend visit to friends who had just moved to a popular resort town, a van carrying three people inexplicably crossed the line dividing the two-lane road and slammed into the front of the vehicle on the passenger's side. Kathryn, who had been driving, was seriously injured and Gerald was killed instantly. As she told her psychologist some weeks later, "When I came to I was kind of hazy, but I looked over and knew he was dead. I couldn't even recognize him."

Although there were many difficulties that Kathryn brought to counseling, including significant depression and multiple symptoms of posttraumatic stress, a central issue for her was simple. "Why would God let this happen to Gerry and me"? Prior to Gerald's death, they both had shared what she later described as a "fairly simple Biblical faith. I tended to believe that righteous people prosper and God protects them. Well, we had tried to live right, and we believed, and we had faith, and look what it got me. Before, things made sense, and the purpose of my life was clear—to live a Christian life and follow Jesus. These days nothing makes much sense to me at all anymore. Life is just pretty much of a big, black, empty hole." During one early session, she looked directly at her therapist and asked, "So how is it possible for me to continue to believe in a good and loving God when he treats his children like he treated me and Gerry?"

As was the case for Kathryn, trauma can produce spiritual damage and a sense of estrangement from God (McBride, 1998). Working with persons who have faced major tragedies means the clinician must deal with spiritual and religious matters. Such issues are not relevant to all individuals, and the specific content varies widely depending on the person's worldview. A major operating assumption that we articulated in chapter 1 is that trauma shakes the foundations or invalidates significant elements of the individual's way of understanding the world. Concurrent with the distress and disruption produced by trauma, the encounter with major loss also offers a great opportunity for the client to change in positive existential or spiritual ways. This chapter examines how the clinician might respond when these themes emerge in therapy. As you consider the description of Kathryn's loss, how would you respond to Kathryn's question and what issues are raised by that question for the counselor? How might clients experience posttraumatic growth in this area? This chapter examines religious, spiritual, and existential issues, but the primary focus is on spiritual and religious themes in therapy with persons in the wake of trauma. It focuses primarily on client belief systems that involve the view that at least some form of transcendent reality exists. However, even persons who have spiritual or religious beliefs must still come to terms with the fundamental questions raised by the existentialists.

There currently appears to be a resurgence of interest in the social psychology of religion and spirituality and a concomitant shift from the use of the word *religion* to the word *spirituality*. As we use them, these words have overlapping, but somewhat different, meanings. *Religion* describes a system of "beliefs, values, and practices" organized around beliefs about God or a transcendent force (Mahrer, 1996, p. 435) that are associated with organized social structures. *Spirituality*, on the other hand, describes the individual's experience of the transcendent, a higher force, or an existential state beyond the self.

EXISTENTIAL ISSUES AND LIFE WISDOM

Themes identified by clinicians working within the existential tradition provide a useful summary of some of the fundamental matters that may be of concern to many clients in their struggle with tragedy (an excellent summary of this general paradigm for therapy is provided by Yalom, 1980). Included in the fundamental, ultimate concerns of human beings are the following: We are mortal and must face death, one's life quest is ultimately each individual's own responsibility, and finding meaning and purpose in life are of central importance for each person. Although existential theorists suggest that these themes may often appear in disguised forms in client's words and dreams, our experience has been that clients dealing with trauma often raise them explicitly.

Many of the kinds of events that lead clients to seek help may involve direct reminders of human mortality. Clearly, this is the case with Kathryn's tragic situation. For other clients, the "intimations of mortality" are more indirect (e.g., when the diagnosis is of serious life-threatening illness or when one has survived a horrible accident or criminal assault). From the existentialist point of view, the human being's status as mortal may be a driving force for psychological problems (Yalom, 1980). The confrontation with one's eventual death also may serve as a powerful stimulus for personal growth. As individuals struggle to come to terms with traumatic events, the naked realization of the limitations of one's existence may be the catalyst for positive changes in one's philosophy of life.

A major assumption of the existential perspective is that each individual is essentially alone in the universe and each person has responsibility for "creating one's own self, [and] destiny" (Yalom, 1980, p. 218). A central experience of many persons facing life crises is the sense of being disconnected from other persons. As the plentiful research on social support has suggested (Schreurs & de Ridder, 1997), positive connections to other persons can be psychologically useful to persons facing stressful circumstances. However, the existential point of view can serve to remind the clinician that concerns over one's ultimate aloneness can produce psychological distress and maladaptive behavioral patterns. Conversely, recognition and acceptance of one's aloneness can also offer the opportunity for major positive changes in one's philosophy of life.

Another emphasis of the existential tradition is the centrality of the quest for purpose in life. "What is the meaning of my life?" is viewed in this framework as perhaps the single most important question for human beings to answer (Frankl, 1963). Although this specific question is not raised by all persons who face trauma, common issues raised are: Why did this happen? Why did this happen to me? What sense does this make? For many persons, these more specific questions relate directly to the general question about the meaning and purpose of life. As individuals in the aftermath of trauma search for understanding of these matters, the clinician may have an opportunity to help the client more fully answer the fundamental existential question of the purpose of his or her individual life.

Although not directly connected to the existential perspective, the work that has been done in recent years on wisdom (Baltes & Smith, 1990) suggests some parallel points of focus. One of the components of wisdom suggested by psychologists who have been studying its development in older adults is the recognition that life is fundamentally unpredictable and that "one can *never* know everything about a problem or an individual's life" (Baltes & Smith, 1990, p.103). In addition, wisdom involves the knowledge of strategies for managing life's uncertainties and, equally important, knowledge about how to live one's life. Perhaps no set of circumstances confronts individuals so clearly with the need to accept the indeterminacy of life, and offers so readily the opportunity to learn how to live life, as encounters with major threats to one's well-being and security. Traumatic events offer one a forced opportunity to change one's general philosophy of life in ways that move one in the direction of greater wisdom.

Learning to engage in dialectical thought is another way in which individuals develop life wisdom. "Dialectical thought … is the ability to recognize and work effectively with contradictions" (Daloz, Keen, Keen, & Parks, 1996, p. 120). As suggested in chapter 1 and elsewhere (Tedeschi & Calhoun, 1995), there are a variety of ways in which the confrontation with suffering leads individuals to increase their ability to use and develop comfort with apparent contradictions. For example, one may need to learn that one has new limitations, as well as new possibilities, one can do less in some ways but more in others, and one has experienced major losses but also gains. Perhaps the most widely quoted summary of life wisdom in the United States is the "serenity prayer" written by the Protestant theologian, Reinhold Niebuhr: "God grant me the strength to change the things I can, the serenity to accept those I cannot change, and the wisdom to know the difference." For some persons in the wake of trauma, the new way of thinking may lead them to see, paradoxically, that they must accept what is, but also to change what has been.

Traumatic events raise existential issues and they may offer the possibility of an increase in life wisdom. The worldviews of many psychotherapy clients in the United States include important spiritual or religious elements. Clearly this is not the case for all individuals. Although the focus of this chapter is on spiritual and religious elements in posttraumatic growth, this discussion may prove useful as a means of helping even clients who are strongly committed atheists, but a radically different semantic framework would be required in that case.

RELIGIOUS SYSTEMS ON SUFFERING
AND MEANING

The major established religions of the world include attempts to answer the major existential issues and the problem of suffering in particular. We turn to a brief and simple overview of some of those points of view as a way of briefly illustrating the kinds of spiritual frames of reference that clients dealing with trauma may have.

In the rabbinical period of the Judaic tradition, and in some elements of the Islamic tradition, there is the view that individuals who suffer are chosen by God. Individuals who suffer are being tested by God, but the selection also implies that the individual is special in some way. Suffering can be a blessing bestowed by God to draw people closer to Him. Suffering can also be a blessing because it may be a means of atonement, even for advancement in some way (Bowker, 1970). The biblical figure, Job, is chosen to suffer because he is viewed as a good man, and his painful experiences serve as messages from God.

A central element in the Christian tradition is the importance of the suffering of Christ. A main element of traditional Christian creed statements is that God ordained the suffering and death of Jesus, and they served the central purpose of atoning for human sin and to reconcile humanity to God. Although some Christian perspectives imply that God sends suffering to chasten individuals and pain is sent as a teacher, others view suffering in a different light. Although suffering may have the consequence of bringing individuals closer to God and increasing the individual's wisdom, life's tragic difficulties are not seen as the doing of God. Suffering may increase humility and wisdom and bring individuals closer to God, but the Christian New Testament does not record Paul as saying that his suffering was a blessing; indeed, "A thorn given to me in the flesh, a messenger from Satan, to harass me for being too elated" (Hoyt, 1978, p. 76).

Some elements of the Hindu tradition view one's suffering in life as a result of one's fate. One's fate is determined by how well one has lived previous lives prior to one's current incarnation. Suffering ends when one is freed from the cycle of birth and rebirth and one no longer needs to participate in the continuing cycle of birth, death, and rebirth. A central challenge is to live a good life within the constraints of the life into which one is born, because the suffering and challenges one must face are the predetermined consequences of how well or how poorly one has lived one's previous lives.

From a Buddhist perspective, suffering is universal and appears to be inescapable. The causes of suffering need to be removed by ethical and compassionate action. Therefore, one should confront suffering directly, embracing it. In addition, Buddhist tradition teaches that detachment from the world is a main avenue for avoiding suffering. Attachment to the world of materials and things contributes to suffering, so a means to reduce one's suffering is to detach oneself from that which contributes to suffering.

These brief, oversimplified descriptions provide some examples of the kinds of assumptions that religious clients may have in struggling to come to terms with major life trauma. However, even individuals who adhere strongly to all of the central assumptions of any particular religious or spiritual tradition can differ widely in how they each understand the spiritual significance of life crises.

THE CLIENT'S SPIRITUALITY AND RELIGION IN THE AFTERMATH OF TRAUMA

Therapists, Clients, and Spirituality

To some degree, the typical citizen and the typical psychotherapist are members of different cultures. This seems definitely to be the case in the United States. The vast majority of Americans view themselves at least in some ways as religious, and they also describe themselves as believing in God in some form. However, some major figures in the history of psychotherapy have taken active antireligious stands (e.g., Freud, Albert Ellis). Mental health clinicians are more likely than the typical citizen to describe themselves as agnostics or atheists and less likely to describe themselves as active participants in organized religion. For example, a survey conducted some years ago indicated that more than half of psychiatrists were either agnostics or atheists (cited in Galanter, 1996). The typical U.S. citizen is likely to consider him or herself religious, whereas the average therapist may not.

However, the spiritual dimension of life is viewed as important by a significant number of American psychologists (Owen, Calhoun, & Tedeschi, 1993; Richards & Bergin, 1997; Shafranske, 1996). Although it is true that practicing psychotherapists are more likely to be agnostics and not to be affiliated with traditional religious institutions, a rather large proportion of American clinicians consider their own spiritual lives important. Interviews with one sample of psychotherapists indicated that, although they tended not to hold conventional religious beliefs, a high proportion reported belief in at least some form of higher power or transcendent reality (Owen et al., 1993). In addition, a majority of American psychologists tend to view religion as valuable, but a minority view religion as an undesirable element in life (Shafranske, 1996).

The available data suggest that, although not inevitable, a clash of cultures on spiritual matters is possible when the typical client consults the typical psychotherapist. Given that existential and spiritual issues are likely to be raised for clients dealing with crisis, a consideration of how to approach these issues in therapy becomes even more important in the context of posttraumatic treatment.

Which Type of Therapist Are You?

There are three general frames of reference that the clinician can have regarding religious matters. One frame of reference can be described as *antireligious* (Pargament, 1997). Psychotherapists with this orientation are firm in their conviction that there is no higher power of any kind, they are atheists, and they view religion as essentially pernicious and undesirable. Religious matters are assumed to be out of place in counseling and treatment should not involve, in any way, religious resources. Freud would clearly fall into this category because, for him, religion was essentially a set of neurotic defenses that the patient should be encouraged to overcome.

A second frame of reference that clinicians can bring to therapy might be described as the *true believer* or the *religious exclusionist* (Pargament, 1997). This perspective assumes there is one single truth in spiritual matters, that the therapist has that truth, and that truth should guide the professional's responses in therapeutic practice. This point of view represents only a small minority of contemporary U.S. professionals and tends to be viewed by many other clinicians as undesirable and unethical (Owen et al., 1993).

The third frame of reference, and the one that we find most appealing, probably represents the majority position among U.S. clinicians: *pragmatic religious constructivism* (Pargament, 1997). The philosophical foundations of the constructivist perspective imply that no absolute reality exists. Regardless of whether such absolute reality is rejected, most practicing clinicians tend to interact with clients at least as if the client's construction of the world is as valid as the clinician's. This would seem to be the case particularly with spiritual or religious matters. Hence, we use the modifier *pragmatic* to suggest that, even if the clinician him or herself does make certain assumptions about ultimate truth, the best way to approach the client is to work within the client's construction of the world. Hence, when spiritual and religious matters are integral elements of the client's understanding of personal tragedy, it is desirable for the clinician to enter, respectfully, into the client's religious worldview and help him or her utilize his or her own spiritual understanding to recover, grow, and develop.

In some ways, antireligious and religious exclusionist therapists are similar because both make certain absolute assumptions that are likely to directly affect how they proceed with clients dealing with major life stressors. To the extent that clinicians taking either of these points of view are paired with clients who share their philosophical and religious assumptions, then no problems would be expected. When such pairing does not occur, then problems might be anticipated. Given the current pattern of popular beliefs, at least in the United States, it would be expected that the antireligious therapist in particular would find a clash of perspectives occurring frequently with clients.

The viewpoint adopted in the following discussion is pragmatic constructivism. Our assumption is that the clinician needs to approach the client's religious or spiritual construction of the world (including those of agnostics and atheists) with respect, accept that construction as valid for that person, and work from that particular framework in encounters with that client. We are not suggesting that therapists who are antireligious or religious exclusionists cannot do good psychotherapy. We are suggesting that clinicians operating within those two viewpoints will encounter more difficulties in working with the typical client facing traumatic circumstances and that those clinicians need to be continually aware of the need to refrain from imposing a certain perspective on the clients they treat.

In Kathryn's case, clinicians who regard religion as undesirable could have difficulty maintaining neutrality about her religious orientation or might even view her spiritual issues as undesirable elements that require modification. The religious exclusionist will have problems, depending on the degree to which a match exists between therapist and client perspectives. The pragmatic constructivist perspective, however, allows the clinician to work with Kathryn within her understanding of life and within her framework of life meaning, reducing the possibility that the clinician will actively work to modify arbitrarily the client's chosen understanding of the world.

SPIRITUALITY, RELIGION, AND COPING
IN THE AFTERMATH OF TRAUMA

Spirituality Can Help

The domain of spiritual matters is not always relevant to clients. As the demographics imply and our clinical experience confirms, a significant proportion of individuals who encounter trauma think about and try to deal with spiritual and religious matters. There are a variety of ways in which religion and spirituality can be helpful to clients in crisis.

For individuals who are a part of organized religious groups, the religious community can be a helpful source of support in times of crisis (Pargament, 1997; Wuthnow, 1994). The religious community can provide social support in the form of emotional support, social activities and social rituals relevant to the specific crises (e.g., funerals); in some contexts, there may be the direct provision of services or material goods. One Christian congregation, for example, has a nurse on staff whose responsibilities include keeping regular contact with aged members of the congregation, helping them to make arrangements and providing direct care when illness creates significant problems for them.

The assumptions that one's life is safe, predictable, and controllable are swiftly negated by events such as the loss of one's house in a fire, a diagnosis of breast cancer, or a motor vehicle accident. As mentioned earlier, a major reason for the highly distressing psychological consequences of life trauma appears to be this major disruption of one's worldview. Fundamental existential and spiritual beliefs, however, are rather robust and difficult, if not impossible, to negate with empirical evidence. One's belief in God, for example, although not immune to assault by what happens in life, is not directly contradicted by any set of life circumstances. Similarly, the existential view that a major driving force for humans is one's eventual encounter with, and current fear of, death is also not easily disproved by what happens in life.

Hence, fundamental beliefs in the spiritual domain, can provide one means for the individual to cognitively assimilate major life disruptions. To the extent that the preexisting belief system allows the individual to restore cognitive balance, reestablishing the foundations of the assumptive world that has been shaken by a seismic life event, then spiritual beliefs can be helpful to the individual in the coping process (Overcash, Calhoun, Cann, & Tedeschi, 1996). There is plentiful evidence indicating that religious and spiritual coping can be helpful to individuals dealing with major life disruptions (see Pargament, 1997, for a comprehensive overview).

Sometimes Spirituality Can Hurt

A Brazilian proverb says that "any religion is good." However, the available data suggest that this is not necessarily the case. As we examine the role of spiritual issues in counseling, from the point of view of assisting the client toward posttraumatic growth, a brief look at the negative role of spirituality in coping seems appropriate. Given the robustness of religious assumptions to disconfirmation by life circumstance, those assumptions and the participation in supportive communities can be quite helpful to the individual. A key element appears to be the specific qualities of the spiritual explanations and interpretations that individuals make about their difficult circumstances.

In Kathryn's case, for example, a conclusion that she seems to have reached is that she and Gerald on the one hand, and God on the other, had an implicit contract. If they lived the right way, then God would take care of them. However, she believes she and Gerald kept their part of the bargain, but God did not. She seems to imply that God is not dependable and trustworthy as she believed. If Kathryn is indeed engaged in such a pattern of thought, is it going to be a negative or positive coping strategy?

The empirical data suggest that at least two forms of religious coping can be harmful to psychological adjustment. One form of harmful coping involves the response of the group to the affected individual; the other involves the individual's spiritual conceptualization of what has happened (Pargament, 1997). The psychological adjustment of individuals who are part of a spiritual community may not be helped or may even be made worse when that community engages in actions that create social costs and deficits for the individual. For example, individuals who report that their religious communities have offered opposition to a chosen course of action in dealing with a problem, or have actively criticized the individual's coping attempts, also report lower levels of psychological functioning (Pargament, 1997). The data suggest, not surprisingly, that when the religious group to which the client belongs engages in social responses that are negative or hostile toward him or her, the individual is worse off for being part of that religious group.

Another way in which spiritual attempts to cope may prove to be negative for the individual's overall adjustment occurs in the individual's spiritual understanding of the traumatic circumstances. If the individual views the trauma as something God should have prevented but "which He let happen anyway," as a sign of abandonment by the higher power, or as a "way of punishing me for my sins and lack of spirituality" (Pargament, 1997, p. 299), then psychological adjustment is adversely affected. Spiritual attempts at coping, then, although they are helpful in many instances, are negative in some. From an empirical viewpoint, there are some religious interpretations that clients make that may be undesirable when the criterion used is level of psychological distress and maladjustment. How is the clinician to distinguish good from bad spiritual understanding?

The Client'S Spirituality: Good or Bad for Posttraumatic Growth?

Two colleagues who are practicing psychotherapists read the earlier summary of Kathryn's situation and an interesting conflict of interpretations occurred. One reacted negatively to the summary and indicated that the portrayal of her religious faith clearly indicated an immature and unsophisticated perspective, and that many readers would be offended by it. The other colleague indicated that he thought this was an excellent case for the chapter beginning because it raised many of the issues that were being addressed in the chapter. The two colleagues were, among other things, making judgments about whether Kathryn's religious views were good or bad. How does the psychotherapist decide whether the individual's religion is good?

At this point, some readers of this discussion may reach the conclusion that the question is arrogant, inappropriate, and perhaps even unethical. The assumption is that the psychotherapist must remain neutral in matters of values. Neutrality, in our view, is generally the goal of choice for the clinician. However, even established professional ethical codes make value judgments about some forms of client behavior (American Psychological Association, 1992). Our view is that, although it is imperative that the clinician do everything possible to avoid manipulating the client's views and choices, psychotherapy is never an entirely ethically sterile enterprise. There is perhaps no other situation in psychotherapy that is as value-laden as when the client wrestles with spiritual or religious themes in the aftermath of a major crisis. Given that some spiritual interpretations may prove detrimental to the client's general psychological adjustment, we return to the question: How does the psychotherapist decide whether the individual's religion is good?

First, we want to make a disclaimer. This question is one that may not be answerable at all. Certainly it cannot be thoroughly addressed in brief form, as a brief detour on the way to a discussion of posttraumatic growth and spiritual issues in therapy. However, we offer three general ethical rules of thumb that offer some vantage points from which to evaluate the client's spiritual interpretations. The three rules of thumb are: (a) what about the common good, (b) what about the client's development as an individual, (c) what about moderation in all things?

The notion of the *common good* is a slippery one, because different groups of individuals, particularly in highly diverse societies such as is typical in North America, will reach quite different descriptions of what that common good is. The general ethical question is this: To what extent would this course of action contribute or detract from the common good? If the individual's religious interpretations and spiritual understanding lead to conceptualizations and actions that tend to contribute to the common good, then one might regard them as good. Daloz et al. (1996) suggested that "the common good would include such core elements as global scope, a recognition of diversity, and a vision of society as composed of individuals whose own well-being is inextricably bound up with the good of the whole" (p. 16). Kubler-Ross (1997) also referred to this principle in citing what she learned from persons who reported near-death experiences. She found that a common aspect of the "life review" with God that occurs near-death is being asked the question, "What service have you rendered?", and that the ultimate lesson to be learned is unconditional love.

A second rule of thumb is a consideration of the extent to which the client's spiritual understandings contribute to his or her own personal development and psychological growth. Does an individual's interpretation that her breast cancer is punishment from God because she has "been a woman of weak and wavering faith" contribute positively to her well-being and development? When a father views the death of his newborn son as punishment for his promiscuous premarital sexual behavior, should the psychologist accept or support that understanding? As with the general notion of a common good, the idea of psychological development and growth is also difficult to establish. Nevertheless, it can be useful for clinicians to at least give consideration to this general question as they work with persons struggling with crisis who try to come to a spiritual understanding of what has happened.

The third general consideration is probably familiar—it is the principle of the *golden mean*. The classical formulation goes back to the ancient Greek philosopher Aristotle. As with the previous two general rules of thumb, the idea is simple, but its specific implementation is not always clear. A central assumption on which the golden mean rests is that the ethical and virtuous path is the one between extremes. The middle course is assumed to be better than either extremes of excess or deficit. In our rather simplified version of the golden mean, the rule of thumb is simply that, in the context of spiritual beliefs in general, and religious beliefs and actions in particular, the golden mean lies between the extremes of fanatical devotion on the one hand and categorical and hostile rejection of spirituality on the other. As with our other two rules of thumb, however, the specific application of the principle still requires the judgment of the psychotherapist in the specific clinical circumstance. We now turn to the main focus of the chapter—posttraumatic growth and spiritual issues in counseling.

POSTTRAUMATIC GROWTH AND SPIRITUALITY AND RELIGION IN PSYCHOTHERAPY

What Should Therapists Know About Spirituality or Religion?

The short answer to the question is: a lot. Unfortunately, the typical program of clinical training does not include much attention, if any, to dealing with spiritual or religious matters raised by clients. However, clinicians whose clients regard spiritual matters as important or relevant to their traumatic situation need to know much in this domain. To be appropriately comfortable with these issues in therapy, clinicians should study the religions and spiritual systems of their clients even if they are not themselves religious at all. No therapist can know everything, of course, and no therapist can develop the necessary familiarity with the cultural and spiritual traditions of every client. Nevertheless, the more therapists know about spirituality and religion, the better able the clinician will be to assist clients as they face very difficult circumstances and nurture posttraumatic growth in the spiritual domain.

Working with traumatized clients can raise challenging questions about existential issues and spiritual matters for the clinician. In the context of religious beliefs, it is important for the clinician to have either worked through his or her own issues in this area or at least be genuinely aware that these matters are still unresolved. When clients experience existential distress and anxiety triggered by a traumatic event, (e.g., impending death), to what extent does this make salient for the therapist his or her own failure satisfactorily to come to terms with the inevitability of death?

What Does the Therapist Need to Know About the Client's Spirituality?

We currently live in the southeastern United States. Some colleagues of ours who have moved here from other parts of the country have reported that they were somewhat bewildered when one of the first questions new neighbors asked them was, "what church do you go to?" This question may also bewilder some clinicians. However, for clients who are coping with the consequences of major life trauma, an examination of spiritual practices and belief systems is desirable. Although inventories and questionnaires about spirituality or religious coping may be useful for research purposes, our experience is that they do not add much for clinical work with individual clients. Whichever assessment path the clinician chooses—clinical or psychometric—he or she must approach this domain with great tact. On most occasions, direct inquiry can prove useful (see Pargament, 1997, for a more detailed description of how this process might unfold). To what extent do you see yourself as a spiritual/religious person? and To what extent have you been thinking about spiritual or religious issues? are examples of probes that can prove useful. Although we are not necessarily advocating that one conduct a spiritual assessment during the first intake session, we are suggesting that the clinician be alert to opportunities to find out more about the client's spiritual and religious perspective. If the clinician is going to work toward facilitating growth for the client in this area, then knowledge of the client's views and experiences in this area is important.

It may also be useful if the clinician can develop an early understanding of the degree to which spiritual beliefs have been shaken, shattered, or already modified in the wake of trauma. Although spiritual assumptions appear to be more robust than empirical assumptions about the world, many persons experience some degree of challenge to important philosophical assumptions. Having a good sense of what the individual's spiritual beliefs were before, what they are now, and which important assumptions are still being ruminated about can be helpful in attending to the spiritual issues that emerge in counseling.

Attending to Spirituality in the Client and Posttraumatic Growth

One of the most important elements in good psychotherapy may be how well the psychotherapist listens to the client. Because the domain of spirituality is one in which individuals can experience significant posttraumatic growth, it is important for the clinician to attend and listen carefully for spiritual and existential themes. The clinician should listen for the themes and attend to them when they occur, identify the theme when it is there, and label it. What we are suggesting is quite simply that the clinician exemplify accurate empathy in the spiritual domain and that he or she not shy away from identifying such themes when they occur. If you were with Kathryn when she articulated the views summarized at the beginning of the chapter, it would be obvious that she was talking about religious issues. However, these themes are not always so obvious.

The father of a young man who committed suicide sought help because of a serious depression occasioned by his loss. In an early session, he said, "I just keep going over and over in my mind what role I played in this. Maybe I should have reconciled with his mother. Maybe I should have worked fewer hours. Maybe this is somehow a result of how I have lived my life. Maybe I just should have been a better person."

Of course, there is no single correct next response for the therapist implied by this short example. The client's words imply either spiritual or existential issues. What we are saying is simply to pay attention when those themes emerge and do not ignore them. In this situation, the therapist's response was: "You are struggling with a lot of very burdensome and gnawing unanswered questions about Ricky's death. One big implied question seems to be, how should I change the way I live my life?" The content of this exchange is not explicitly religious, but the clinician is attending to existential and spiritual elements. The response helped the client focus on the general theme of how to alter life priorities and how to make new choices, which is often a major way in which clients report posttraumatic growth.

Posttraumatic Growth and Spiritual Issues in Therapy

We have already suggested that in an early session, perhaps even the first one with clients struggling with traumatic events, the clinician obtain information about this domain. It is also appropriate to probe about spiritual issues when they seem relevant in context. Sometimes it is useful to draw out religious or spiritual issues directly or at least test to see if they are there.

> *Therapist*: I'm wondering if there are any particular religious views you have that you use to understand this situation?
>
> *Client*: Sure, but I thought counselors didn't think much of that sort of thing.
>
> *Therapist*: I think anything you are relying on to handle this is important. Would you tell me about the religious part?

The clinician working with the father described earlier at one point asked, "How does Ricky's death fit in with how you understand why things happen in life?" What the client began to talk about subsequently was his upbringing in a very traditional Catholic family and his change of beliefs as he had grown older. He currently was an atheist, but he felt that he needed to pursue what he described as a godless form of spirituality in which one should seek "peace and enlightenment" by simply "doing what is right in life."

There are innumerable spiritual and existential themes that the therapist should attend to and probe for, and some of the common themes include: issues related to mortality, life's purpose and meaning, one's life priorities, fundamental choices about how to live, issues related to traditional religious beliefs and expressions, and broad spiritual themes. Sometimes the client's response suggests that the particular spiritual understanding the client has of his or her problem is one that, in the clinician's judgment, may be "bad." For example, the individual's understanding is not only one that suggests the absence of posttraumatic growth; in addition, it is one that may contribute to poorer psychological adjustment. How should the therapist approach the matter?

To encourage posttraumatic growth in the spiritual domain, and to be most helpful to the client, psychotherapists must be capable of offering alternative views to the client. We are fully aware that we are making a recommendation for going out to skate on very thin ice. Some clinicians who make the assumption that psychotherapy can and should be completely value neutral will find this recommendation highly objectionable. However, even those who assume that psychotherapy can never be completely sterilized of values will be concerned, and appropriately so, about the possibility for abuse or misjudgment by the therapist. We strongly agree that one must proceed with great caution in this arena.

A Protestant clergyman once remarked, "The only honest way in which I should try to convert another person to my own viewpoint is if I am just as open to be converted to his viewpoint as I want him to be to mine." Some degree of self-disclosure on the part of the therapist about spiritual points of view that are different from those of the client may be desirable (recall the three suggested general rules of thumb), and perhaps even necessary, for the possibility of posttraumatic growth to be enhanced in the spiritual sphere. As with self-disclosure about anything, self-disclosure by the psychotherapist about spiritual matters must always "be in the service of the growth of the patient" (Yalom, 1980, p. 414).

In addition, the clinician needs to be continually aware of the power differential in clinical relationships. Offering an alternative perspective to clients must be approached, as with all interactions with clients, with humility. The clinician must also convey the perspective in such a way that the client has the behavioral freedom to accept or reject the alternative without even the perceived risk of losing the support and acceptance of the psychotherapist.

At the summary at the beginning of the chapter, Kathryn asked the question, "So how is it possible for me to continue to believe in a good and loving God when he treats his children like he treated me and Gerry?" The psychologist working with Kathryn was familiar with her general religious belief system, had done a significant amount of study about religion in general and her form of Christianity in particular, and had herself wrestled with the general question of how a good God can allow so much suffering to occur. She felt comfortable with religious issues and, in her judgment, it would be appropriate to gently, tentatively, and respectfully offer a differing perspective. Her response to Kathryn's question was: "You are struggling with an issue that is very tough. I am not sure I know how I would answer your question with absolute certainty, but I guess I tend to think that perhaps God did not want either you or Gerry to suffer." What ensued was an exchange between therapist and client on the elements of Kathryn's religious views with which she was struggling and an examination of alternative views that Kathryn had already been considering.

Helping the client survive, cope, improve, or, in some cases, recover is the main focus of psychotherapy with persons who are facing major life stress. Within that context, the opportunity may arise for clinicians to help clients grow in ways that might not have been possible if they had not been forced into the posttraumatic struggle. One of the avenues for growth is existential or spiritual development. For posttraumatic growth to be more likely, the clinician must be knowledgeable about, comfortable with, alert to, and active in working with the client's spiritual issues. For example, the clinician needs to be different than, the early psychoanalytic ideal of the blank slate therapist. The clinician must venture into value-laden areas where many of us feel a certain degree of professional queasiness. To work effectively with clients who struggle with spiritual issues in the wake of trauma and enhance the likelihood that growth will occur, it is desirable for the psychotherapist to develop some degree of comfort in the roles of philosopher and spiritual guide. To repeat, this must always be done in the service of the client's well-being and growth.

Countertransference Matters and Posttraumatic Growth

In traditional psychoanalytic theory, countertransference refers to the process whereby psychotherapists may play out unconscious conflicts in relationships with clients. In the value-laden domain of spirituality and religion, clinicians must maintain continual vigilance so that their responses are not fueled by their own needs. Psychotherapists working with clients to enhance the possibility of posttraumatic growth must be aware of the biases they have about religious and spiritual issues as well as their own personal philosophies of life. They must be continually aware of how they are responding, moment to moment, to clients as they articulate their responses in the spiritual sphere.

Recall the reactions of the two colleagues to the summary of Kathryn's tragic loss. One colleague viewed Kathryn's theological perspective as immature, whereas the other simply thought of the description as a helpful case for discussion. To the extent that the first colleague's views are characterized by some degree of antipathy for religiously conservative views, how might that particular personal stance affect his or her reaction to Kathryn's question? Would there be approval or disapproval, a desire to help her move toward a more sophisticated version of religious beliefs, a temptation to educate her, or perhaps even a need to expound on why her interpretation would lead to poorer coping and lowered psychological adjustment?

As Rogers (1961) suggested many years ago, good therapists must be fully and genuinely aware of their true experience moment to moment in psychotherapy. The clinician's overt response to the client, however, must always be guided by the goal of doing what is best for the client. When helping clients explore posttraumatic growth in spiritual matters in the aftermath of trauma, following Rogers' suggestion is of crucial importance to the practicing clinician.

What Is a Good Spiritual Outcome in Posttraumatic Growth?

The ultimate arbiter of posttraumatic growth in spiritual and religious matters is the client. If the individual's struggle with trauma leads him or her to experience a better understanding of spiritual or existential matters, if the individual experiences a strengthening of freely chosen spiritual commitments, if the individual undergoes an increased sense of purpose and meaning, or if the individual selects a new and better life course, then there has been a good outcome. We are making the assumption that the choices and changes are good. However, even if they are not (unless there are unambiguous ethical violations), if the individual experiences the outcomes described then posttraumatic growth in the spiritual domain has occurred.

Other sections of this book discussed ways in which growth and distress may coexist. In no other domain of posttraumatic growth is this more true. There may well be an inevitable dialectic between distress and growth and between illusion and truth. Individuals who are highly

successful at coping with trauma and are able quickly to muster sufficient resources and defenses to reduce their distress may be less likely
to experience spiritual growth. Individuals whose fundamental philosophies of life are only slightly shaken by traumatic events may be less
likely to experience spiritual growth than those individuals whose spiritual belief systems cannot readily assimilate and quickly defend
against the gnawing existential questions that are made salient by the
confrontation with suffering, loss, and death. To help a client grow in
the aftermath of tragedy, the clinician must not withdraw from helping
the client confront the ultimate difficult questions of life. Paradoxically,
the clinician must also be respectful of the positive illusions that protect
the client from extreme distress.

Homework

For Clinicians

1. Identify your own spiritual, religious, and existential perspectives. One source that may be useful is the religious orientation scales
developed by Batson, Schoenrade, and Ventis (1993). There are four
scales that assess the following areas: doctrinal orthodoxy, the degree to
which the individual views religion as a dynamic quest, the degree to
which the individual's beliefs are influenced by external social forces,
and the degree to which the individual's religious views are the result of
internal personal factors. The greatest utility for the practicing clinician
is simply reading the items and introspecting about the degree to which
such considerations are personally important, and perhaps the
self-identification of areas of spirituality that may be emotionally
charged.

2. Another useful personal exercise for the psychotherapist may be
to simply sit down and write an autobiographical summary of one's individual spiritual and existential history. What was the religious life of
your family of origin, what was your socialization in the area of spirituality, what salient events are connected to how your sense of meaning in
life has developed, and what are your current answers to the fundamental existential questions. In particular, what do you currently see as
the meaning and purpose of your life? To the extent that these kinds of
exercises raise difficult or painful issues, then seeking professional consultation for yourself may prove beneficial.

3. Give some consideration to the crises that you have personally experienced. Think about the degree to which existential or spiritual issues were central elements for you as you struggled with your own
personal difficulties. To what extent did you experience posttraumatic

growth in this area? What negative consequences are you still experiencing from the trauma?

For Clients

The exercises described for clinicians might be adapted for clients as well. In addition, the following can be used to good effect with some clients.

1. *Automatic writing.* In this assignment, the client engages in a meditation by posing a question or an issue and allowing a response to come through his or her writing. For example, a client might pose questions such as, "What is it I am supposed to take from all this?" "Is there some reason I'm going through this?" The clients must be able to give up control of his or her responses to some force that comes from beyond an conscious understanding. This usually takes practice over a number of writing sessions.

2. *Being still.* Another way to allow new perspectives to emerge is to encourage clients to engage in some other form of meditation where the question of meaning or purpose is repeated silently for several minutes until a response or idea begins to emerge. Where responses emerge from is not for the therapist to judge. Some clients experience messages from God, others messages from themselves, and still others messages from deceased loved ones. We leave this for the client to understand.

3. *The life review.* The goal of this exercise is twofold: (a) to highlight the principles that people are using to live their lives, and (b) to make the principles more of a conscious choice—a discipline. As Kubler-Ross (1997) has said, "Ultimately, each person *chooses* whether he comes out of the tumbler crushed or polished" (p. 193); (italics added). Although it is impossible to create the life review described by Kubler-Ross and others, who have heard this reported from hundreds of people, a minor approximation can be helpful. It is also highly confrontative and as Kubler-Ross (1997) said, could be interpreted as " ... heaven or hell. Maybe both" (p. 192).

Clients are asked to consider the path of their lives by reflecting on how they have chosen to live according to certain principles.

Step 1: Randomly (through a sort of free association) select five incidents in your life. Do not censor what comes to mind, but allow them to present themselves—no matter how minor or major they seem.

Step 2: What was your most basic motive in choosing to do what you did in each situation?

Step 3: In each incident, how well did you love—unconditionally, without regard for yourself, and without judging the other?

Step 4: How did you serve?

Of course this assignment demonstrates a certain spiritual stance, (i.e., unconditional love and service represent the highest forms of living), and this assignment should only be given to clients who are ready to confront themselves on this level. This is not an assignment meant to demonstrate to clients that they are immoral, hypocritical, or the like. Also, we invite clients to choose their own incidents so that certain important issues they may already be engaging can be confronted more directly.

7

Posttraumatic Growth:
Issues for Clinicians

This chapter focuses on issues that individual therapists may confront in their work with persons who have experienced tragic or extremely challenging sets of life circumstances. A question that is asked about clinical work in general, and sometimes crisis work in particular, is: Do you have to have experienced the crisis to help others cope with it? Is it necessary for the individual therapist to have experienced at least some kind of crisis to be able to assist individuals toward recovery, as well as enhance the possibility that posttraumatic growth may occur?

There is at least one way in which having been there yourself may be helpful: It may enhance your credibility with your clients. A group of persons who had experienced the suicidal death of a loved was asked about the ways in which others had been of help to them after their loved one died (Wagner & Calhoun, 1991). An interesting comment was made by several of the participants in the study. Although they described people in general as having tried to be supportive, it was other persons who had experienced a similar loss of a loved one to suicide who were perceived as the most helpful. It is likely that a similar process may operate in clinical work. Clients may view therapists who have experienced similar traumas as being in a more advantageous position to understand them than clinicians who have not shared similar experiences.

Clinicians who have experienced similar traumas and who have also undergone posttraumatic growth as a result may have the additional advantage of already having experienced the perspective change mentioned in chapter 1. These clinicians are already attuned to the possibility of positive change arising from the struggle with crisis and may have

125

an easier time noticing, labeling, and reinforcing it, compared with therapists who have not undergone similar experiences.

Despite the potential advantages for the therapist, as is seen later, there also may be some disadvantages for trauma therapists who have been exposed to trauma. Our view is that having gone through similar experiences is not necessary for the clinician to be effective in creating the possibility for posttraumatic growth. The main ingredients are for the clinician to be effective generally, engage in the kinds of psychotherapeutic strategies that are most helpful to the individual client, and attend to the possibilities of growth in the words and actions of the client.

THE EFFECT OF TRAUMA WORK ON THE CLINICIAN

Negative Effects

There are several terms that have been coined to identify the negative impact of trauma work on the therapist; for example, *vicarious traumatization* (Pearlman & Saakvitne, 1995), *compassion fatigue*, and *secondary traumatic stress disorder* (Figley, 1995). The particular pattern of therapist distress would be expected to vary with a variety of factors, including the types of crises that clients relate to the clinician, the proportion of clients that are coping with traumatic events, and the degree to which clients' experiences include exposure to the kinds of horrible, emotionally shocking circumstances that would place any individual at risk for stress-related psychological difficulties (Pearlman & Saakvitne, 1995).

Early in this book we described the role that traumatic events play in shaking or shattering the foundations of the individual's worldview. The therapist who is working with a person who has experienced such events can also experience, vicariously, the shaking or shattering of the foundations of his or her own worldview. Along with the experience of having one's construction of the world called into question by the client's account, it may be possible for the empathetic engagement with the client to create significant levels of psychological distress in the therapist.

When clients describe experiences that involve physical harm to themselves or others, clinicians may become concerned about their own safety or the safety of loved ones (McCann & Pearlman, 1990). The psychologically comfortable assumption that one's own individual world is safe may be contradicted for the clinician by the evidence described by the client. A young woman sought an appointment with a psychologist because she was having difficulty coming to grips with the death of her fiancée in a motor vehicle accident. Not only was the loss devastating, but the circumstances were particularly traumatic. She had survived the crash, but he had been killed instantly, violently, and gruesomely. As she related her horrible experience, the psychologist became significantly stressed by what he heard. In the days following, he began to worry about members of his family when they drove off to school and work, and he began to call frequently on the car phone to check to make sure they were fine; he would become noticeably anxious about their welfare if they did not call him to report that they had arrived safely at their destinations. Fortunately, the psychologist's excessive worry and anxious checking began to dissipate after a consultation session with a colleague.

People also tend to assume that they have some significant amount of control over what happens to them (Janoff-Bulman, 1992; Taylor, 1989). There are individual differences in the degree to which this assumption is held, but the experience of a major crisis reduces the sense of control for most persons. The therapist, who listens to accounts of events such as the motor vehicle accident, may also experience a reduction in the general sense of control over daily life. A general sense of "they couldn't prevent it and maybe neither can I" may develop. The clinician described earlier clearly experienced a loss of his sense of safety; he was engaged is some rather maladaptive strategies to ensure that loved one's were safe in situations that he clearly was not able to control.

The clinician can also experience a range of distressing emotions in response to the client's descriptions. Just as the emotions of sadness, depression, anger, and anxiety are common among individuals facing crises directly, the therapist can also experience these unpleasant emotions as a result of empathic engagement with the client (Pearlman & Saakvitne, 1995). The psychologist's response to his client's account of her fiancée's sudden death clearly includes a significant amount of anxiety. One might reasonably have expected the clinician to experience sadness at the tragic loss of a young life, as well as anger at the generally unjust set of circumstances that produced it.

Following such descriptions of tragic circumstances, therapists may also experience some of the more intense symptoms of stress-related syndromes, including intrusive thoughts and images. These would seem more likely for clinicians who work with clients who relate extremely intense and distressing experiences, where the clinician is able to visualize the events the client is describing.

There are a wide variety of terms and concepts that have been used to describe the phenomenon whereby therapists exposed vicariously to trauma become distressed, as well as the negative impact the clinician's work can have (e.g., burnout). There is a word of German origin that seems to at least metaphorically summarize the central elements of the general concept of therapist burnout, as well as the more specific experience of vicarious traumatization—*welschmerz* (i. e., a general state of pessimism and melancholy about the state of the world). Chessick (as cited in Pearlman & Saakvitne, 1995) described the *soul sadness* that clinicians can feel. Mental health workers in general are susceptible to professional burnout, but trauma workers can face the additional risk of significant distress produced by the highly demanding nature of the work. Whether it is thought of as vicarious traumatization, soul sadness, or a general weariness about the world and one's work, the risk is there for clinicians who provide clinical support to persons facing serious life crises.

Risk Factors

The factors that have been identified as placing clinicians at risk for problems triggered vicariously by their clients' experiences can be summarized in three general categories: severity of exposure, duration of exposure, and individual vulnerability.

The severity of exposure for the clinician parallels the factors that determine severity of exposure for the client. Clients who have experienced serious threats to themselves or their loved ones, who have experienced catastrophic destruction in their vicinity, who have been exposed to horrible scenes of violence, or who have witnessed the suffering of children (Figley, 1995) may bring accounts that present particular risk for the therapist. The more horrible the experience of the client, the greater the risk of vicarious negative impact on the clinician.

Duration of exposure also seems to be a risk factor (Pearlman & Saakvitne, 1995). The greater the proportion of a caseload that consists of persons with traumatic histories and the longer the clinician practices with trauma clients, the greater the risk of negative reactions. Clinicians whose work is almost exclusively composed of trauma recovery work are particularly at risk for vicarious negative responses (Herman, 1992).

Clinician vulnerability also plays a role in the risk of secondary distress (Neumann & Gamble, 1995; Pearlman & MacIan, 1995). Beginning clinicians may be at higher risk than experienced clinicians. Beginning clinicians face a variety of stressors unrelated to trauma work per se (e.g., adapting to new organizational and occupational challenges and roles, learning how and in what ways they are effective healers, and usually beginning in lower levels of status than experienced clinicians). The added challenges of work with clients facing highly demanding life situations may seriously challenge or overwhelm the beginning clinician's coping abilities.

Clinicians who are trauma survivors may also be at greater risk than clinicians who are not (Pearlman & MacIan, 1995). This may be the case especially when clients experience raises unresolved issues for the therapist. For example, clinicians who are survivors of severe childhood sexual and physical abuse may find themselves becoming overwhelmed with anger toward the perpetrator of the abuse that a client has experienced. If the therapist shows inappropriate anger in a session with a client or experiences increased irritability with loved ones, vicarious negative reactions may be manifesting themselves.

Positive Effects: Vicarious Posttraumatic Growth

The potential negative effects of clinical work with traumatized clients have been identified and studied (Figley, 1995; Pearlman & Saakvitne, 1995), but no similar body of inquiry exists for the potential vicarious positive effects of working with clients in crisis. There have been some initial attempts to discuss and study the positive impact of trauma work (Arnold, 1998; Saakvitne, 1997; Schauben & Frazier, 1995). Based on what others have related and on our experience as clinicians, we suggest some ways in which the clinician may experience posttraumatic growth vicariously through the secondary experience of the therapeutic engagement with clients and their struggles with extreme life stress.

One way in which clients may change therapists is simply through their own accounts of heroic struggle and survival. Their courage and survival may inspire us as clinicians (Pearlman & Saakvitne, 1995). The simple knowledge that the client was exposed to horrible circumstances, was not destroyed by them, or in some way experienced growth in the struggle may provide a chance for clinicians to regard human beings in general, and perhaps themselves in particular, as stronger than they had ever imagined possible. As Pearlman and Saakvitne (1995) suggested, the " client's courage and determination may inspire us to press forward in our own continuing personal growth" (p. 404).

At the same time, however, the client's story may show us that we are all potentially vulnerable to tragedy and loss. Clinicians may learn to understand more fully the paradoxical dialectic that clients learn. The empathic understanding by the clinician can lead him or her to realize that, as human beings, we are more vulnerable to loss than we had hoped, but we are also stronger than we had imagined possible. As the client's struggle with overwhelming difficulty unfolds, the clinician may become more able to appreciate the inevitable reality that life offers the possibility of trauma, but also that there are strengths that are discovered and developed in the struggle with those traumatic events.

Sometimes this truth that we are all vulnerable becomes reality and the lessons learned from our clients who are trauma survivors can be especially useful. A friend and colleague with whom one of us has conducted parental bereavement support groups for years recently confronted the death of her own child. She recognized that working with bereaved parents for many years provided a certain advantage. She had seen people survive this, so she had hope for herself. She had seen the diverse ways people cope and knew that she could choose her ways from all that she had learned. She was used to confronting pain in others, allowing herself the freedom and courage to confront her own. Despite all this, she knew she had to go through the pain anyway.

Clinical work with persons dealing with major crises can also offer the opportunity for clinicians to experience positive changes in their worldviews and general philosophies of life. Trauma work can challenge worldviews and lead to negative changes, but there is also the possibility of vicarious growth as the client's experience leads clinicians to reexamine their own general philosophies of life. Existential issues are often salient for the client (see chap. 1 and 6), and the client's focus on them may raise these issues for the therapist as well.

The process whereby the client's struggle raises existential issues for the clinician is not necessarily pleasant for the therapist. It is good for the clinician to confront the fundamental questions of existence (Yalom, 1980), but when these matters become salient they may well raise the clinician's level of psychological discomfort. Confronting these issues is necessary; to the extent that the clinician addresses them openly and honestly, that can be regarded as an important element of vicarious posttraumatic growth.

A common element of posttraumatic growth is the experience of a reevaluation and shift of life priorities. As clinicians listen to the traumatic experiences of their clients, they can find themselves thinking about their own life priorities and making some conscious choices about what is important to them. For example, working with groups of bereaved parents, frequently makes group leaders who have not lost a child more aware of how time with one's own child is precious. This awareness can lead to a conscious choice to spend more time with one's own family and children. Each time clients talk about the loss of their child, the clinician is again reminded of what his or her own priorities need to be.

Closely connected to the experienced positive shift in life priorities is the vicarious lesson that one must appreciate each day more. "I have learned simply to appreciate each day" is a common theme in the experience of persons dealing with a wide variety of traumatic events (Tedeschi & Calhoun, 1995). A similar process can operate in clinicians. Clinicians can be stimulated by the client's difficulties to be more appreciative of many elements in life. There are numerous possibilities: (a) the clinician who is assisting an abused wife may become more grateful for a supportive and compatible spouse, (b) the clinician who is providing support to an adult survivor of child sexual abuse may become more appreciative and grateful for the good elements of her own family of origin, (c) the crisis worker who works with the homeless can become more appreciative of her own modest apartment, (d) and the therapist who specializes in work with abused children can recommit himself to being a good father to his own children, perhaps working harder to control his irritability even when he is under significant stress. As one colleague put it, "working with a client who is facing really difficult things usually leads me to do my own priority check, and when I do that I inevitably appreciate my own situation more, at least in some way."

The direct struggle with crisis can lead individuals to experience a stronger connection to other persons. The clinician's vicarious experience of that struggle can produce similar changes. "When I go home after doing a group," one leader of support groups for grieving parents said, "I hug my kids just a little bit harder." The vicarious experience is often one in which the clinician more fully realizes the degree to which maintaining and nurturing connections to others is important. There is the greater appreciation of loved ones, but clinicians may be induced by the client's experience to strengthen their own ties to other persons. "You appreciate them more, but you also want to work on keeping those connections and making them deeper and better"

The familiar line from the English poet John Donne, "no man is an island," reflects another avenue for vicarious posttraumatic growth in therapists. Clinicians, through their work with clients struggling with the aftermath of major stressors, may begin to experience an empathetic connection to all human beings who suffer (Pearlman & Saakvitne, 1995). The clinician's own sense of general compassion for fellow human beings can increase as a result of trauma therapy work. Clinicians can experience on a daily basis the gentle reminder of their connection to others who experience pain and tragedy, which is the mixed blessing of feeling compassion for other human beings who face difficult, sometimes horrible circumstances. In the John Donne phrase, trauma therapists know "for whom the bell tolls."

Work with survivors of major life crises can raise important existential questions for the therapist; it can also make salient the connection to other persons, particularly those who suffer. This combination of heightened existential awareness and enhanced sense of connection to other people may lead some therapists to find a significant purpose as socially active participants in life. One clinician who specializes in working with adult survivors of child sexual abuse is actively involved in political action to increase programs designed to prevent child abuse; he also routinely participates in marches and other activities in support of rights for gay and lesbian persons. Another clinician, who works occasionally with clients posttrauma, actively works within the organized structure of her church to improve race relations and increase the acceptance of gay persons into the clergy. The clinician's active participation in actions designed to provide support to persons who suffer or face difficult challenges may be initiated by the experienced connection to other persons that is generated in the work with clients in crisis. In turn, the participation in actions designed to improve things may add a significant element to the clinician's sense of purpose and meaning in life.

The Cosmic Slap: Use the Opportunity

We have suggested that the possibility of posttraumatic growth begins when the foundations of the individual's worldview are severely shaken or shattered. The vicarious experience of the client's struggle gives the therapist the opportunity of experiencing a controlled shaking of the foundations without having to pay the high price that the client pays. The therapist's engagement with clients, and with clients' own experience of shattered worldviews, will allow the therapist to, vicariously, experience growth in the perception of self and other persons, philosophy of life, and relationships with other persons.

Actor and comedian Richard Belzer has described cancer as a "cosmic slap in the face." The clinician who works with persons who have been cosmically slapped by life crises is given the opportunity to attend to some important life issues without having to directly experience the sting and pain of that slap. Clinicians should be prepared to identify, label, reinforce, and encourage posttraumatic growth in themselves just as they do with clients. The clinician must attend to that possibility and take advantage of the opportunity provided by the empathetic engagement with clients who have directly confronted a variety of cosmic slaps.

FOUNDATIONS THERAPISTS NEED

To enhance the possibility of posttraumatic growth in clients, there are important philosophical and spiritual foundations the clinician needs. Perhaps the most simple and easily achievable foundation is to have as great and as deep a knowledge as possible of the kinds of worldviews clients have. There has been a welcome increase in recent years in the importance of attending to cultural differences among clients and the role of differences between clinicians and clients (American Psychological Association, 1993). To assist clients in moving toward posttraumatic growth, such understanding is crucial.

The easiest avenue to general knowledge about clients' worldviews is to read about and actively study them. Clinicians need to read about the religious, spiritual, and philosophical traditions from which their clients come. A simple example involves obtaining knowledge of the world's major religious traditions. Although such broad knowledge does not make the clinician a knowledgeable participant in those religious and cultural traditions, such knowledge does provide a useful framework for understanding individuals whose experiences occur within the framework of those traditions. To put it more broadly, what are the paradigms and perspectives about life and how to live it that are likely to have influenced the clients whom you are going to treat?

The answer to that question, in the context we currently do our clinical work, might be roughly summarized with the label *moderate to conservative Protestant Republican*. There are two obvious general perspectives summarized by that compound label: (a) the Protestant branch of Christianity in its moderate and conservative manifestations, and (b) the political tradition of the Republican Party in the United States. Our assumption is that we as clinicians will be more effective if we have a good understanding of the values and assumptions that clients who come from those traditions are likely to have.

Given that the general U.S. population tends to be somewhat more *religious* than the population of American mental health professionals, knowledge of the mainstreams of American religious thought may be particularly useful for therapists to have. As seen in chapter 6, this type of knowledge may be even more important when working with clients in crisis, but it is clearly more relevant to some client groups than for others. As the demographic and cultural landscape of the United States changes in the next few years, clinicians are likely to encounter a wider array of different cultural and spiritual perspectives in their clients. For clinicians to be in the best position to encourage posttraumatic growth in their clients, they must have familiarity with a wide range of spiritual and philosophical foundations.

Although all clinicians know this already, a reminder seems appropriate. The crucial knowledge that clinicians need is of the individual client's worldview, not simply abstract knowledge about general systems or perspectives. We have observed in some clinicians the admirable quality of wanting to become familiar with cultures different from their own to better serve their clients. However, this can sometimes lead the clinician to respond to the client as simply a member of a particular cultural or ethnic category, rather than as a unique individual who may come from a particular cultural tradition but with his or her own unique and idiosyncratic perspective. Although we are advocating greater general knowledge about cultures and systems of belief and thought, we are at the same time adding the caution that it is the individual person that the clinician must respond to, not the individual's cultural or spiritual category.

Much of what clients experience as posttraumatic growth occurs within the parameters of their philosophies of life, particularly their understanding of how the fundamental existential questions about mortality and the meaning of life are answered. The more clinicians know about clients' understanding of how those questions are answered, the more effective they will be in enhancing the possibility of posttraumatic growth.

Clinicians working with trauma survivors often have a sense of honor and privilege in being able to hear the horrific stories. These stories are not shared with most people, and trust is evident in survivors choosing to share them. When survivors share the details of such pain, it is an honor to be chosen to hear it. This honor involves getting close to the soul of the client—the place of greatest vulnerability. The honor is also the raw honesty in clients who are choosing to share secrets and pain. There are few, if any, times in usual social discourse where such honesty is allowed. Even clients' intimates may not hear these stories because clients may feel a need to protect them. Therapists are privy to the most intense emotion, the most distressing memories, and the most closely guarded secrets. In such a trusted position, therapists can learn what it means to be human.

Just as readers and audiences may be affected by biographies or performances of tragedy, and reconsider their views as a result (Tedeschi & Calhoun, 1995), empathic clinicians are almost inevitably affected by stories of trauma and survival told by their clients. However, these stories are more likely to be emotionally affecting because the survivor is present and the story may be private.

Trauma tends to force clinicians to consider their own fundamental views of the life well lived. In addition, it questions why some people suffer, either by blind chance or at the hands of another human? It is useful to actively reflect on these issues and get used to talking about them before working extensively with trauma survivors. Some clinicians may have to be desensitized to having such discussions if they tend to be quite private about such things. Trauma survivors are often not shy about asking questions about life's meaning, the reasons why one should continue to live after a trauma, what life priorities should be, how to relate to those who are mired in the apparently trivial, and what kind of God there is, if there is one. It is important for clinicians to feel comfortable with explorations of such existential and spiritual questions; they should be open to various resolutions of them and to living with the lack of resolution. Therapists can short-circuit the process of growth by being evasive on one hand or too sure of the answers on the other. The therapist's job is to invite exploration of such issues by the trauma survivor. We are convinced that supporting such explorations with the sense that the survivor will find a good enough answer for themselves can be a useful part of posttraumatic growth.

It is not necessary for therapists to have figured out all the cosmic details. In fact, it may be better for them to reveal themselves in their spiritual unsettledness so the client is not tempted to adopt the therapist's stance on these beliefs. For example, if a grieving client asks the therapist whether she believes in an afterlife, the therapist might say that she is not sure, but would like to, or that she does, but is not sure what it is like.

In general, therapists who help trauma survivors move toward growth are ideally open to the spiritual elements of the process, actively support these considerations, are willing to consider various perspectives without feeling threatened, and are willing to talk about their own views while making it clear that there is no pressure for the client to adopt them. We believe that this takes someone who has directly confronted his or her own spiritual life and who continues to do so. In fact, we believe that therapists who work most effectively in helping persons grow after trauma are therapists who are still open to growth themselves; they are open to and appreciative of the potential effects of working with each trauma survivor.

CLINICIAN SELF-CARE

Clinicians in general and trauma therapists in particular must attend to the issue of self-care. Clinical work is challenging, and working with clients who have dealt with highly demanding and sometimes horrible events can take its toll on the clinician. For the clinician to be effective generally, and to be most able to encourage posttraumatic growth in clients, he or she must stay in good psychological and physical shape. What follows is a brief summary of some of the actions that therapists can take to reduce the chance of significant negative responses resulting from trauma work. Although these suggestions may be common knowledge, a brief explicit listing may be useful as a reminder for practicing clinicians.

Self-Care As a Professional

No therapist is completely immune to professional burnout, and no clinician who works with trauma survivors is immune to secondary stress
and vicarious traumatization. One important element of self-care in the
professional arena is to recognize that it can happen to any clinician
(Meichenbaum, 1994). It is important for all clinicians to consciously attend, on a regular basis, to their level of overall stress and to the level of
professional stress in particular. Awareness of the possibility and regular self-evaluation are important components of the identification and
prevention of negative reactions.

Perhaps the single most important element in the prevention of negative reactions is the honest acknowledgment that there are limits to the
amount of change and growth that clinicians can help foster in their clients. A concept developed by Rotter, Chance, and Phares (1972) is very
helpful in this regard. Although it has a rather obtuse name, *minimal
goal level*, it speaks directly to the clinician's need to be realistic regarding expectations of positive change in clients (Cerney, 1995; Pearlman &
Saakvitne, 1995). Minimal goal level refers to the minimal level of per-
formance that an individual perceives as satisfactory. For example,
what is the minimal level of progress or posttraumatic growth in a client
that you would regard as reflecting good therapeutic work on your
part? More generally, what minimal level of improvement in your clients would you regard as indicating you are a good therapist? The likelihood of negative therapist reactions increases as the minimal level of
growth and improvement the therapist regards as successful is raised.
The more unrealistically high the expectations are, the greater the likelihood of therapist disappointment and negative self-evaluation. As negative self-evaluation persists, one would expect increased vulnerability
to therapist stress reactions and professional burnout. Clinicians' expectations should be realistic, but clinicians also must consciously notice when things go well—when clients show improvement and growth
(Pearlman & Saakvitne, 1995). It is important to notice and consciously
identify positive change in clients. When clinician expectations are realistic and clinicians work systematically to note even small indicants of
adaptive coping or growth, then negative clinician reactions are less
likely.

Regular supervision or consultation with colleagues are also important. All clinicians benefit from regular consultation with colleagues.
However, clinicians who may be especially vulnerable to burnout or vicarious traumatization should make sure that they have regular consultation or supervision from experienced colleagues. Beginning
clinicians, clinicians who have survived major life trauma, and clini-

cians whose caseloads include a high proportion of severely trauma-tized clients should seek regular supervision. Any clinician who is working with even one client who has been exposed to extreme life stress should seek consultation with appropriate professional col-leagues.

Another step in professional self-care is to limit the overall caseload and carefully consider the mix of clients in the caseload (Meichenbaum, 1994). It varies among clinicians, but every clinician has a limit to the size of caseload that can be handled satisfactorily. In general, the bigger the caseload, the more likely the clinician is to experience negative reac-tions. Where caseloads are heavy, clinicians need to be particularly care-ful about monitoring their own level of professional stress and engaging in preventive self-care. The mix of types of problems in thera-pists' caseloads is also an important consideration. Therapists whose work is done primarily or exclusively with persons who have under-gone extremely traumatic experiences are probably more vulnerable to burnout and vicarious traumatization than clinicians whose caseloads include only a small and intermittent number of highly traumatized cli-ents. Individual clinicians need to monitor the mix of client problems in their caseloads and manage the mix as they consider best for them.

Personal Self-Care

The recommendations in this section are even more widely known than the prior ones. However, despite this general knowledge, many clini-cians do not engage in actions that prevent negative therapist reactions. Following are reminders of actions that most clinicians know about, but in which they may not be actively engaged. Although these elements of personal self-care do not directly address the specific experience of sec-ondary stress or vicarious traumatization, they serve to increase one's ability to withstand stress. These suggestions represent ways in which clinicians can improve the quality of their protective armor. Engaging in good professional self-care will not reduce the level of stress to which they are exposed, but self-care may reduce the likelihood that the stress to which they are exposed will cause noticeable negative therapist reac-tions.

Regular vigorous, aerobic exercise is a useful component in profes-sional self-care. Of course, it must, be appropriate to one's health and physical condition, and individuals should not begin programs of vig-orous exercise without appropriate medical consultation. Regular exer-cise has a variety of physical benefits. For clinician self-care, the more noticeable benefits may be psychological. Regular exercise can reduce anxiety and depression, and it can also increase one's general sense of psychological well-being (Mutrie, 1997).

Proper nutrition and adequate sleep are also important components of self-care. The simple reminder is to eat right and get enough sleep. Not atypically for the average American professional, clinicians may be most likely to eat improperly during the middle of the day. Clinicians should beware of developing patterns of clinical practice that do not include appropriately nutritious food and an appropriate amount of time to eat it during lunchtime. For clinicians who consume foods or beverages containing caffeine, it is important to avoid their use in ways that might interfere with adequate sleep.

Clinicians also need to take breaks from their clinical work, including vacations, and to build barriers to protect their personal time away from clinical work. To the extent that is it practical, they need to erect barriers between themselves and their clinical work. One simple, useful practice is to utilize transition activities between the professional world of clinical work and the personal life away from the professional demands (e.g., changing clothes from professional attire to the attire of the home).

Once, in a stress management workshop one of us was conducting, a nurse who was a participant began to smile as the discussion focused on transition activities between work and home. During the next break, she said that previously she had not realized the direct impact of those activities, and she described her own experience with transition activities. She was a single parent with a 9-year-old son and she typically arrived home from work soon after her son had arrived from school. He would not speak to her when she came in the door in her nurse's uniform. After she had changed her clothes to *civilian* wear, he greeted her warmly by repeating, "Hi, Mom. Want some tea now?" Prior to her transition activity of changing clothes, she was *the nurse*; after she changes, she was *Mom*.

Make sure that your personal life includes recreation, relaxation, and play (Pearlman & Saakvitne, 1995). A colleague who conducts stress management workshops is fond of saying that "anything worth doing is worth doing *wrong!*" Clinicians should try to find activities that are unrelated to their professions and that are inherently restorative and enjoyable, regardless of their particular proficiency at them. If the enjoyable activities also provide an opportunity for self-expression, even better. We know clinicians who play soccer, play musical instruments, make tape-recorded musical "mixes" for friends, have an herb garden, read mystery books, do mediocre carpentry, and greatly enjoy coaching youth softball. There are infinite possibilities—find some for you.

The restorative power of nature can also help reduce stress and improve one's general resilience to it (Yassen, 1995). Even for persons who do not particularly like the outdoors, we suggest at least making some attempt to seek whatever aspects of nature are appealing and available. Possibilities range from overnight backpacking trips in remote areas to simply sitting on a bench in a *green area* in the middle of a large city.

Seek good humor and share it with friends and colleagues. Although much has been written about the stress-reducing and stress-managing aspects of humor, we have a word of caution. First, all humor is not created equal. In general, it is desirable to avoid humor that insults or deprecates individuals or groups. Second, although some humor involves silliness, there is a difference between acting stupid and being humorous. Wearing a big nose and large red shoes may be funny in some contexts (e.g., to small children), but it is probably not a good way to introduce humor into the clinical workplace. In some ways, humor may have the same ability that poetry does—it conveys feelings that individuals may not have been able to put into words. Seek out and share humor that is constructive; in particular, search for humor (e.g., cartoons, jokes, quotes from comedians) that addresses professional issues representative of current clinical work. It is important to remember that you do not have to be funny yourself to utilize humor as a means of professional self-care. Cultivate your own ability to perceive humor in difficult circumstances. If you want to share humor, do what Arnie Cann, a colleague and researcher on humor (Cann, Calhoun, & Banks, 1997), recommends: Do what all the best comedians do for their funny stuff —*steal it!*

A final suggestion is also common knowledge among clinicians, but its importance suggests we include it as a reminder too. Work to develop and maintain supportive relationships with others at and away from work. In particular, it is a good idea to make sure that the support system outside of work is diverse and not composed solely of clinicians. Although throughout this section we know that we are, as the saying goes, *preaching to the choir*, in the domain of relationships we want to add some additional preaching. A general belief that is common in our culture is that relationships should develop and continue spontaneously. The corollary to this belief is that consciously working on relationships is somehow engaging in manipulation—something that is viewed as undesirable and perhaps even immoral. Clinicians are unlikely to agree with this irrational way of thinking. However, it is important for clinicians to be reminded to consciously attend to the important relationships in their lives and maintain and nurture those relationships.

Homework for Clinicians

1. Evaluate the degree to which you have experienced vicarious posttraumatic growth from your work with clients who have faced highly stressful situations. What positive changes, if any, have you perceived in yourself as a result of your work with trauma survivors?

   Changes in self-concept?
   Changes in philosophy of life, spiritual life, or religious life, including life priorities, gratitude, and appreciation for what you have or simply for what is?
   Changes in relationships with others?

2. Conduct an inventory of your own self-care. Following is a list of the sample of self-care recommendations made in this chapter. Look at each and evaluate whether your current life includes it; determine any changes that might be useful for you to make to enhance your level of both professional and personal self-care.

   Professional Self-Care

   Vicarious traumatization and secondary stress reactions—any present?
   Examine your own expectations for satisfaction in your work—how realistic are they?
   Evaluate the size of your total caseload—what modifications does it need?
   What proportion of your caseload is composed of severely traumatized clients? What modifications might be needed?

   Personal Self-Care

   How much and how appropriately are you exercising?
   Evaluate your current nutritional and sleep habits.
   How successful have you been at using transition activities, taking time off, and building appropriate barriers between work and you?
   How much playing, recreating, and relaxing have you been doing?

How adequate for you is your current level of immersion in nature?

How effectively are you using humor currently?

Evaluate your current support system at work and away from work.

How diverse is your support system away from work? What have you been doing to nurture relationships at work and away?

8

Resources for Clinicians and Clients

Chapter 5 discussed how important connections with others can be in the experience of posttraumatic growth. Sometimes these connections can be made through the writings of people who have endured trauma and who describe how they have been affected. Such books can be inspirational, but the ones recommend here do not downplay the anxieties, anger, and pain that must also be endured. That is important, because, as was said before, people who have gone through trauma have often heard from their share of people with easy answers. We usually find the autobiographical accounts most illuminating, but sometimes these are too much for some people to get through. This chapter offers some suggestions for reading. This is certainly not an exhaustive list. Fiction, biography, and autobiography offer a wealth of stories about overcoming trauma and about posttraumatic growth. Clients often discover these on their own, and many therapists are well read in this area and have their favorites to suggest. This chapter also has a section on some professional resources that clinicians might turn to for additional ideas on encouraging posttraumatic growth.

RESOURCES FOR CLIENTS

For those who are not avid readers or whose situation does not allow them to concentrate for long periods, we find some little books by Jim Miller quite useful. Miller publishes books and tapes for the bereaved, the incapacitated, the terminally ill, and their caregivers. These books and tapes are often filled with poetry and photographs of nature and are quite comforting. The material for people enduring trauma and loss is hopeful and clearly entrusts coping and decisions to the survivors. Some examples of materials that encourage posttraumatic growth are the videotape entitled *How Do I Go On?: Redesigning Your Future After Crisis Has Changed Your Life* (Miller, 1989) and the audiotape *The Transforming Potential of Your Grief: Eight Principles for Renewed Life* (Miller, 1993) A book that is a meditation on grief and growth is entitled *Winter Grief, Summer Grace: Returning to Life After a Loved One Dies* (Miller, 1995). Miller (1994) presented 12 bits of wisdom in *What Will Help Me? 12 Things to Remember When You Have Suffered a Loss/How Can I Help? 12 Things to Do When Someone You Know Suffers a Loss.* The book is in two parts—one meant for the survivor and one for the helper—and each of the 12 points is covered concisely in two pages. Of particular interest is Point 10: Your time of loss can be a time of soul making unlike any other. He introduced the bereaved to the notion that there may be something in this experience for them:

> The poet Emily Dickinson describes the paradox this way: "A deathblow is a life blow to some ... .". This blow you have been given can put you in touch with life's ultimate mysteries, which can be as beautiful as they are bewildering. It can be a time of awakening you'll never forget. It can lead to a rare event: a life blow. (Miller, 1994, p. 25)

Miller is a clergyman, and there are religious themes and references in most of his works.

In a previous book (Tedeschi & Calhoun, 1995), we described some other works that tackle spiritual elements of lessons that can be learned through trauma. These include C. S. Lewis' (1963) *A Grief Observed*, Rabbi Harold Kushner's (1981) *When Bad Things Happen to Good People*, and Joan Borysenko's (1993) *Fire in the Soul: A New Psychology of Spiritual Optimism*. These represent quite different religious perspectives: Christian, Jewish, and new age, respectively, but they reach similar conclusions about the spiritual development that can occur as one copes with grief. Many people find that religious and spiritual issues become important in a way they had never been, and this often prompts a spiritual quest that can pay off in a more profound experience of the spiritual life.

The stories of trauma survivors found in Robert Lifton's (1993) *The Protean Self; Human Resilience in an Age Of Fragmentation,* Shaena Engle's (1997) *Silver Linings: Triumphs of the Chronically Ill and Physically Challenged,* and William Helmreich's (1992) *Against all odds: Holocaust survivors and the successful lives they made in America* all show how, in the cases of these survivors, putting oneself into action has produced tremendous personal fulfillment and societal benefit. For example, Lifton said that we all relate to the holocausts of our era because of what survivors have shown us, and therefore we all can learn something. He described the *death imprint* that is "experienced as a form of knowledge of death that informs a commitment to life enhancement" (1993, p. 81). Survivors have it and, in some form, so do the rest of us. This is the vicarious growth that is possible for us as clinicians when we have intimate contact with our clients' stories.

There are some books that come close to being self-help books for posttraumatic growth, including *The Survivor Personality* (Siebert, 1996), *Watersheds: Mastering Life's Unpredictable Crises* (Lauer & Lauer, 1998), *The Resilient Self: How Survivors of Troubled Families Rise Above Adversity* (Wolin & Wolin, 1993), and *Seven Choices: Taking the Steps to New Life After Losing Someone You Love* (Neeld, 1990). These books all emphasize active choosing and problem solving, and are therefore best for people some distance from the experience of their trauma, when they are able to be active again. They tend to lack a focus on spiritual issues that often become so important to people who have suffered certain kinds of trauma, or who have questions about living that include this dimension. Of these, Siebert's book most clearly recognizes the possibility for posttraumatic growth. In a section entitled "The Serendipity Talent: Turning Misfortune into Luck," he encourages survivors of misfortune to poke fun at the crisis, experiment with perspective, and ask explicitly how the situation may be useful. His stories that illustrate "survivor personalities" show how some people react to adversity as if it were something they desired.

Another book that is a guide to overcoming trauma is *A Gift of Hope: How We Survive Our Tragedies* by Robert Veninga (1985). Most of the book is crisis intervention and trauma recovery advice, but there is also a chapter on faith that includes something of what we have described as posttraumatic growth. Veninga described people who cope with their trauma by saying "yes" to life. He attempted to clarify that he is not talking about a *shallow optimism*, but "a radical reorientation toward life in which we actively believe that *life can be trusted*" (p. 231). For this to happen, acceptance and meaningfulness must be present. Trusting, acceptance, surrender—saying "yes"—are also found explicitly in spiritual experiences described in Elisabeth Kubler-Ross' (1997) memoir, and in several of Jim Miller's materials.

New life is not just a choice you make—
it is an opportunity you are offered, a gift you are given.
It is not just something you do—it is something you accept.
It is not something you force—it is something you trust.
And in the trusting you encourage your healing.
For the God of all creation,
the Maker of each changing season in nature,

is also the Guide through each changing season of your grief.
What is happening to you is not mere happenstance.
Something larger than you has a word to speak,
and that word is
Yes. (Miller, 1995, p. 43)

Some books that can be helpful for trauma survivors interested specifically in negotiating the difficulties of spiritual renewal and creation of meaning include *Spiritual Crisis: Surviving Trauma to the Soul* (McBride, 1998) and *The Search for Meaning* (Naylor, Willimon, & Naylor, 1994) with its associated workbook. The latter especially has some good writing exercises that can guide survivors to articulate the principles for living their lives that will sustain them in the aftermath of their trauma and serve them well in the future. Survivors can develop an assumptive world that will be able to accommodate whatever comes their way and prepare for a happy death. For example, in the last exercise in the workbook, Naylor et al. referred to ways of life that will lead a person to die unhappy, including separation from others, inauthenticity, and wasting one's life by failure to recognize mortality. However, clinicians should be aware that this material is also written at a level most accessible to those who are well educated and comfortable with existential philosophy, as represented by Albert Camus, Rollo May, and Erich Fromm.

Using stories to illustrate her points, Stephanie Dowrick (1997) showed how the meaningful, well-lived life is constructed out of the virtues of courage, fidelity, restraint, generosity, tolerance, and forgiveness. Her book, *Forgiveness and Other Acts of Love*, can help clients discover or develop the personal qualities that can make trauma survival more meaningful. Our clients can be ripe for a consideration of these issues of virtue when they are searching for something that makes sense in a world that can seem absurd in the aftermath of trauma.

Among autobiographical accounts of posttraumatic growth are some that were written by people who had important influences on the field of traumatology as professionals, especially Victor Frankl and Elisabeth Kubler-Ross. Frankl's (1963) *Man's Search for Meaning* is a well-known classic that shows how an existential understanding of suffering, control, and helplessness can be used to cope with trauma. However, Frankl's book focuses more on living through ongoing trauma than its aftermath.

In *The Wheel of Life: A Memoir of Living and Dying* (Kubler-Ross, 1997), the psychiatrist who is a seminal figure in the treatment of the dying described how she took terrible circumstances, especially in the aftermath of World War II, and created an important life out of them. She repeatedly referred to misfortune and suffering and the growth experiences that followed. When a benefactor went bankrupt and she lost a much wanted position as a lab technician, she said, "As a result of my bad luck, I found the key to my future career" (p.52). She quoted a survivor of a concentration camp who had been determined to survive to tell stories of the horror she had witnessed and, upon liberation, had adopted a new purpose, "If I can change one person's life from hatred and revenge to love and compassion, then I deserved to survive" (p. 78). It also turns out that Kubler-Ross became a psychiatrist because she became pregnant and could not take the pediatric residency she sought. She was left to work in a state psychiatric hospital in a residency that no one wanted. Then she miscarried and said she learned an important lesson: "You may not get what you want, but God always gives you what you need" (p. 111). There are many such instances where it is easy to see examples of people who had turned disaster into benefits. Some of this is hindsight, whereas other examples are of deliberate attempts to find the benefits. Her theme throughout is to prepare for the good death by living lovingly and authentically—the theme also found in the Naylor et al. (1994) workbook. Kubler-Ross also focused on spiritual development in the aftermath of traumas, especially terminal illness and near-death experiences. Her experience and understanding of spiritual matters includes reincarnation, channeling, and the like. Thus this book may be most palatable for clients for whom these alternatives are useful.

In *Living Posthumously*, an account of his attempt to discover the cause for a mysterious, chronic, debilitating illness, Andrew Schmookler (1997), first described the loss of control, the loss of identity, and *comforting illusions*. These losses set the stage for a search for meaning and rebirth. This search includes consideration of many autobiographical accounts of coping with illness and impending death, numerous references to literature, and wonderful stories and humor. This is also a terrific book for clinicians that wish to reap a harvest of tales to pass onto clients.

Reynolds Price (1994) described his bout with cancer and his resulting paraplegia in *A Whole New Life*. He said things that echo Schmookler. For example, in one of our favorite passages from his book, Price wrote that we must grieve for the old self and become "somebody else, the next viable you—a stripped-down whole other clear-eyed person" (p. 183) while Schmookler stated that, "illness can strip a person of his or her abilities, leaving only bits and pieces of the edifice that had been there before. But often the pieces that remain include the essential core of the structure, and a way can be found to preserve the soul of one's old work" (p. 162). Price emphasized the importance of his creativity in dealing with the pain and anxiety surrounding his cancer and the ways others can provide useful support. He was not afraid to critique those who failed him at his time of need, especially some in the medical field. He and Kubler-Ross gave the most damning indictment of failures of compassion, and their suggestions on how to respond to the sick and dying can serve as important self-examinations for trauma therapists as well.

Several traumas strike Diane Cole, which she described in *After Great Pain: A New Life Emerges* (1992). While a college student, she helped her future husband with his battle with cancer. Soon thereafter, Cole suffered the loss of her mother. Then 2 years later, armed terrorists invaded the B'nai B'rith Building in Washington, taking her and more than 100 others hostage for 39 hours of terror. Then she suffered miscarriages and infertility. She described how, after each period of difficulty, "a new self merged, one with a different vision of who I am, a different sense of what I could do or even wanted to do, and a different perspective on what my future might hold" (p. 13)

A useful description of the experience of spousal bereavement can be found in *Doors Close, Doors Open: Widows, Grieving and Growing* by Morton Lieberman (1996). The book is based on the responses of several hundred bereaved spouses to a wide variety of assessments; it was written "for widows and their families" (p. viii). Interviews were also conducted with a smaller sample of widows. Lieberman made liberal use of quotations to illustrate the process of grief and the changes that can occur as widows struggle with their loss. The book includes some quite practical considerations. For example, there is a chapter entitled "Do You Need Psychotherapy?" There is also a chapter on support groups. A unique aspect of the book is the inclusion of a chapter that explicitly addresses the prospects for growth coming from the struggle with grief. This is not a how-to book, but it offers a helpful framework for women coping with the death of a spouse.

In *Tuesdays With Morrie*, Mitch Albom (1997) described his encounters with his former Brandeis professor, Morrie Schwartz, as the latter faces the inevitable physical deterioration and eventual death from amyotrophic lateral sclerosis (ALS). ALS is a progressive neurological disorder that increasingly reduces the individual's ability to control muscles. It had been 20 years since Mitch Albom had last seen his former professor. After seeing Morrie being interviewed about his condition on a national news show, Albom made contact with his old friend and they began a series of regular visits. *Tuesdays With Morrie* is Albom's story of their encounters as Morrie moved closer and closer to death.

The book is short and many will regard it as inspirational. The conversations with Morrie are described on the book jacket as "lessons in how to live." Morrie's *lessons* include his thoughts on marriage, money, death, forgiveness, and saying good-by. The book is not specifically intended for persons facing crises, nor is it designed to directly instruct individuals on how to deal with specific matters. Its accessible writing, inspirational tone, and commonsensical ideas may prove helpful to persons dealing with major life difficulties.

Clinicians should read and evaluate each of the books they intend to recommend to clients to determine the appropriateness of their recommendations. These resources must be used carefully. If a clinician encourages a client to read a book about posttraumatic growth before the client is ready to use it as encouragement, the suggestion could be misinterpreted as indicating the clinician has high expectations or that the client is moving too slowly. It is best to first mention the existence of this kind of literature and let the client indicate his or her readiness to consider it. The clinician can also be quite explicit in telling clients that reading about others' growth experience can inform them about the possibilities, but must not be taken as any kind of demand. For example, when a client is beginning to refer to some important things he or she has learned from coping with the aftermath of trauma, the therapist might say, "What you are saying reminds me of some things other people have told me and some have written regarding their trauma experience. I know of some books about this if you are ever interested in looking at them."

Such readings are not for every client. Others have been profoundly affected by what they have read. The written word can be more powerful for some than the spoken one. We have had some clients tell us that the perspective found in reading has completely changed their outlook, but these have usually been people who have asked, "Do you know of anything good I can read about this?"

RESOURCES FOR CLINICIANS

Clinicians can benefit just as clients can from reading many of the sources mentioned earlier. However, for books that focus on posttraumatic growth, providing explanations, research, theory, or clinical application, the choices are limited. For the clinician who wishes to read more extensively about the research on posttraumatic growth, we know of only two additional books that have been focused on this area. Our first book on the topic was *Trauma and Transformation: Growing in the Aftermath of Suffering* (Tedeschi & Calhoun, 1995), which provides a broad, interdisciplinary overview of posttraumatic growth. *Posttraumatic Growth: Positive Change in the Aftermath of Crisis* (Tedeschi, Park, & Calhoun, 1998), a companion volume to this one, contains chapters by many of the distinguished scholars who are currently examining various issues in posttraumatic growth. Both volumes provide extensive citations and reference lists for individuals.

There are other sources that touch on certain aspects of posttraumatic growth that might be especially useful to clinicians. We divide these into conceptual issues related to posttraumatic growth and therapy interventions of particular use in growth enhancement.

Resources for Conceptual Issues

Janoff-Bulman's (1992) *Shattered Assumptions* provides the cognitive viewpoint of traumatic response that creates the possibility for growth. Another way to view the process of change of worldviews can be found in *The Psychological Meaning of Chaos* edited by Masterpasqua and Perna (1997). This book includes chapters that describe how chaos theory can be applied to understanding the psychotherapy enterprise. A chapter by Mahoney and Moes on "Complexity and Psychotherapy" is particularly useful, showing how trauma sets in motion attempts to achieve a new dynamic balance within a survivor. There is much attention paid to the use of metaphor to understand psychotherapy and how clients use metaphors to describe psychological chaos and restabilization. Other books that focus on metaphor include *Creative Thought: An Investigation of Conceptual Structures and Processes* edited by Ward, Smith and Vaid (1997), Kopp's (1995) *Metaphor Therapy: Using Client-Generated Metaphors in Psychotherapy*, and *Metaphor: Implications and Applications*, by Mio and Katz (1996), which also describes how therapists use metaphor. *Creative Cognition* by Finke and Bettle (1996) also provided a good description of the kind of thinking clinicians might want to encourage in trauma survivors to enhance growth.

Individual Differences in Posttraumatic Response: Problems With the Adversity–Distress Connection by Marilyn Bowman (1997) shows the importance of personal characteristics, such as emotionality and beliefs, in determining responses to trauma; it shows that resilience is the norm. Her arguments fit well with the constructivist position we take and the evidence of posttraumatic growth that we have noted. Carolyn Aldwin's (1994) *Stress, Coping, and Development: An Integrative Perspective* also provides a model of posttraumatic growth in a chapter entitled "Transformational Coping."

Resources for Interventions

There are many books that describe posttraumatic treatment, but they focus on the initial stages of work and symptom alleviation rather than posttraumatic growth. Martin Seligman's (1990) *Learned Optimism* can be a source of ideas for cognitive restructuring and homework assignments. We do not recommend it for use in the treatment of trauma survivors, because the *adversity* in most examples of adversity–belief connections are hardly traumatic. However, clinicians will find many examples of optimistic versus pessimistic explanatory style that they may be able to use with clients.

Although not focused on posttraumatic growth, an example of an approach to positive possibilities for clients that resonates with ours is *Beyond Blame* by Jeffrey Kottler (1994). Kottler showed how therapists can help clients turn certain experiences that can have extremely stressful components toward positive functions, including personal growth. We also recommend that clinicians refer to recent books that show how to integrate religious and spiritual elements into psychotherapy. *A Spiritual Strategy for Counseling and Psychotherapy* by Scott Richards and Allen Bergin (1997), *Religion and the Clinical Practice of Psychology* by Shafranske (1996), and *The Psychology of Religion and Coping* by Kenneth Pargament (1997) are particularly good. Clinicians interested in encouraging posttraumatic growth in clients would do well to integrate elements from humanistic-existential, cognitive-constructivist, and narrative therapy into their models of practice and should consult excellent sources on therapy within these traditions.

CONCLUSION

The general paradigm for treating trauma survivors has been dominated by medical models and by an exclusive focus on symptom removal. We hope that this book is another resource for clinicians—one that will fill a gap in the literature by making salient the importance of promoting the best long-term developments for trauma survivors. It begins with symptom removal, but includes the possibility for encouraging posttraumatic growth as well. Posttraumatic growth is possible perhaps because the majority of trauma survivors are already equipped with a natural tendency to restabilize their systems of comprehending, creating meaning, and developing themselves.

Effective and thorough trauma treatment must recognize this possibility and act to make the most of it.

References

Affleck, G., Tennen, H., & Gershman, K. (1985). Cognitive adaptations to high-risk infants: The search for mastery, meaning, and protection from future harm. *American Journal of Mental Deficiency, 89,* 652–656.

Albom, M. (1997). *Tuesdays with Morrie: An old man, a young man, and life's greatest lesson.* New York: Doubleday.

Aldwin, C. M. (1994). *Stress, coping, and development: An integrative perspective.* New York: Guilford.

American Psychological Association. (1992). *Ethical principles of psychologists and code of conduct.* Washington, DC: Author.

American Psychological Association. (1993). Guidelines to providers of psychological services to ethnic, linguistic, and culturally diverse populations. *American Psychologist, 48,* 45–48.

Arnold, D. (1998). *Vicarious transformation in psychotherapy with trauma survivors: A descriptive investigation of the views of practicing clinicians.* Unpublished master's thesis, UNC Charlotte, Charlotte, NC.

Baltes, P. B., & Smith, J. (1990). Toward a psychology of wisdom and its ontogenesis. In R. J. Sternberg (Ed.), *Wisdom: Its nature, origins, and development* (pp. 87–120). New York: Cambridge University Press.

Baltes, P. B., Staudinger, U. M., Maercker, A., & Smith, J. (1995). People nominated as wise: A comparative study of wisdom related knowledge. *Psychology and Aging, 10,* 155–166.

Batson, C. D., Schoenrade, P., & Ventis, L. W. (1993). *Religion and the individual.* New York: Oxford University Press.

Baumeister, R. F. (1994). The crystallization of discontent in the process of major life change. In T. F. Heatherton & J. L. Weinberger (Eds.), *Can personality change?* (pp. 281–297). Washington, DC: American Psychological Association.

Becker, D. (1998, May 22). Cycling through adversity. *USA Today,* p. 3c.

Bloom, S. L. (1998). By the crowd they have been broken, by the crowd they shall be healed: The social transformation of trauma. In R. G. Tedeschi, C. L.

Park, & L. G. Calhoun (Eds.), *Posttraumatic growth: Positive changes in the aftermath of crisis* (pp. 179–213). Mahwah, NJ: Lawrence Erlbaum Associates.

Borysenko, J. (1993). *Fire in the Soul: A new psychology of spiritual optimism*. New York: Warner.

Bowker, J. (1970). *Problems of suffering in religions of the world*. New York: Cambridge University Press.

Bowman, M. (1997). *Individual differences in posttraumatic response: Problems with the adversity–distress connection*. Mahwah, NJ: Lawrence Erlbaum Associates.

Bradburn, N. A. (1969). *The structure of psychological well-being*. Chicago: Aldine.

Breslau, N., Davis, & Andreski, P. (1995). Risk factors for PTSD-related traumatic events: A prospective analysis. *American Journal of Psychiatry, 152,* 529–535.

Calhoun, K. S., & Atkeson, B. M. (1991). *Treatment of rape victims*. New York: Pergamon.

Calhoun, L. G., Cann, A., Tedeschi, R. G., & McMillan, J. (1998). Traumatic events and generational differences in assumptions about a just world. *Journal of Social Psychology, 138,* 789–791.

Calhoun, L. G., & Tedeschi, R.G. (1989–1990). Positive aspects of critical life problems: Recollections of grief. *Omega, 20,* 265–272.

Calhoun, L. G., & Tedeschi, R. G. (1991). Perceiving benefits in traumatic events: Some issues for practicing psychologists. *The Journal of Training & Practice in Professional Psychology, 5,* 45–52.

Calhoun, L. G., & Tedeschi, R. G. (1998). Posttraumatic growth: Future directions. In R. G. Tedeschi, C. L. Park, & L. G. Calhoun, (Eds.), *Posttraumatic growth: Positive change in the aftermath of crisis* (pp. 215–238). Mahwah, NJ: Lawrence Erlbaum Associates.

Calhoun, L. G., Tedeschi, R. G., & Lincourt, A. (1992, August). *Life crises and religious beliefs: Changed beliefs or assimilated events?* Paper presented at the meeting of the American Psychological Association, Washington, DC.

Cann, A., Calhoun, L. G., & Banks, J. S. (1997). On the role of humor appreciation in interpersonal attraction: It's no joking matter. *Humor: International Journal of Humor Research, 10,* 77–89.

Caplan, G. (1964). *Principles of preventive psychiatry*. New York: Basic Books.

Carver, C. S., & Scheier, M. F. (1998). *On the self-regulation of behavior*. New York: Cambridge University Press.

Cerney, M. S. (1995). Treating the "heroic treaters." In C. S. Figley (Ed.), *Compassion fatigue* (pp.131–149). New York: Brunner/Mazel.

Cole, D. (1992). *After great pain: A new life emerges*. New York: Summit.

Dakof, G. A., & Taylor, S. E. (1990). Victims' perceptions of social support: What is helpful from whom? *Journal of Personality and Social Psychology, 58,* 80–89.

Daloz, L. A. P., Keen, C. H., Keen, J. P., & Parks, S. D. (1996). *Common fire: Lives of commitment in a complex world*. Boston: Beacon.

Davidson, S. (1992). *Holding onto humanity—The message of Holocaust survivors: The Shamai Davidson Papers*. New York: New York University Press.

Dohrenwend, B. S. (1978). Social stress and community psychology. *American Journal of Community Psychology, 6,* 1–15.

Dowrick, S. (1997). *Forgiveness and other acts of love*. New York: Norton.

Engle, S. (Ed.). (1997). *Silver linings: Triumphs of the chronically ill and physically challenged.* Amherst, NY: Prometheus.

Epstein, S. (1990). The self-concept, the traumatic neurosis, and the structure of personality. In D. Ozer, J. M. Healy, Jr., & A. J. Stewart (Eds.), *Perspectives on personality* (Vol. 3, pp. 63–98). Greenwich, CT: JAI Press.

Falsetti, S. A., & Resnick, H. S. (1995). Helping the victims of violent crime. In J. R. Freedy & S. E. Hobfol (Eds.), *Traumatic stress—from theory to practice* (pp. 263–285). New York: Plenum.

Figley, C. S. (Ed.). (1995). *Compassion fatigue.* New York: Brunner/Mazel.

Finke, R. A., & Bettle, J. (1996). *Chaotic cognition.* Mahwah, NJ: Lawrence Erlbaum Associates.

Frankl, V. E. (1963). Logotherapy and the challenge of suffering. *Review of Existential Psychology and Psychiatry, 1,* 3–7.

Frankl, V. E. (1963). *Man's search for meaning.* New York: Pocket Books.

Frazier, P., & Burnett, J. (1994). Immediate coping strategies among rape victims. *Journal of Counseling and Development, 72,* 633–639.

Freedy, J. R., & Donkervoet, J.C. (1995). Traumatic stress: An overview of the field. In J. R. Freedy & S. E. Hobfol (Eds.) *Traumatic stress—from theory to practice* (pp. 3–28). New York: Plenum.

Fromm, E. (1947). *Man for himself.* New York: Holt, Rinehart & Winston.

Galanter, M. (1996). Cults and charismatic group psychology. In E. P. Shafranske (Ed.), *Religion and the clinical practice of psychology* (pp. 269–296). Washington, DC: American Psychological Association.

Girolamo, G., & MacFarlane, A. (1996). Epidemiology of PTSD: A comprehensive review of the international literature. In A. J. Marsella, M. J. Freedman, E. T. Gerrity, & R. M. Scurfield (Eds.), *Ethnocultural aspects of posttraumatic stress disorder* (pp. 33–85). Washington, DC: American Psychological Association.

Gluhoski, V. L., & Wortman, C. B. (1996). The impact of trauma on world views. *Journal Of Social And Clinical Psychology, 15,* 417–429.

Gomes, P. (1996). *The good book.* New York: William Morrow.

Green, B. L. (1990). Defining trauma: Terminology and generic stressor dimensions. *Journal of Applied Social Psychology, 20,* 1632–1642.

Greenberg, M. (1995). Cognitive processing in trauma: The role of intrusive thoughts and reappraisals. *Journal of Applied Social Psychology, 25,* 1262–1296.

Helmreich, W. B. (1992). *Against all odds: Holocaust survivors and the successful lives they made in America.* New York: Simon & Schuster.

Herbert, T. C., & Cohen, S. (1993). Stress and immunity in humans: A meta-analytic review. *Psychosomatic Medicine, 55,* 364–379.

Herman, J. L. (1992). *Trauma and recovery.* New York: Basic Books.

Hodgkinson, P. E., & Stewart, M. (1991). *Coping with catastrophe.* London: Routledge.

Horowitz, M. J. (1986). *Stress response syndromes* (2nd ed.). Northvale, NJ: Jason Aronson.

Hoyt, T., Jr., (1978). What can Christianity do for me? In H. J. Young (Ed.), *Preaching on suffering and a God of love* (pp. 73–77). Philadelphia: Fortress.

Janoff-Bulman, R. (1989). Assumptive worlds and the stress of traumatic events: Applications of the schema construct. *Social Cognition, 7,* 113–136.

Janoff-Bulman, R. (1992). *Shattered assumptions*. New York: The Free Press.

Jaycox, L. H., Foa, E. B., & Morral, A. R. (1998). Influence of emotional engagement and habituation on exposure therapy for PTSD. *Journal of Consulting and Clinical Psychology, 66*, 185–192.

Joseph, S., Williams, R., & Yule, W. (1993). Changes in outlook following disaster: The preliminary development of a measure to assess positive and negative responses. *Journal of Traumatic Stress, 6*, 271–279.

Joseph, S., Williams, R., & Yule, W. (1995). Psychosocial perspective on posttraumatic stress. *Clinical Psychology Review, 15*, 515–544.

Kelly, G. (1969). Personal construct theory and the psychotherapeutic interview. In B. Maher (Ed.), *Clinical psychology and personality: The selected papers of George Kelly* (pp. 224–264). New York: Wiley.

Kessler, R. C., Sonnega, A., Bromet, E., Hughes, M., & Nelson, C. B. (1995). Posttraumatic stress disorder in the national comorbidity survey. *Archives of General Psychiatry, 52*, 1048–1060.

Komp, D. M. (1993). *A child shall lead them: Lessons in hope from children of cancer.* Grand Rapids, MI: Zondervan.

Kopp, R. R. (1995). *Metaphor therapy: Using client-generated metaphors in psychotherapy.* New York: Brunner/Mazel.

Kottler, J. A. (1994). *Beyond blame: A new way of resolving conflicts in relationships.* San Francisco: Jossey-Bass.

Kubler-Ross, E. (1997). *The wheel of life: A memoir of living and dying.* New York: Scribner.

Kushner, H. S. (1981). *When bad things happen to good people.* New York: Avon.

Kussmann, L. (1997–1998). Wayne's story: An interview one year after becoming paralyzed. In *Aquarius Productions catalogue* (pp. 36–37). Sherborn, MA: Aquarius Productions.

Lauer, R. H., & Lauer, J. C. (1988). *Watersheds: Mastering life's unpredictable crises.* New York: Ivy Books.

Lewis, C. S. (1963). *A grief observed.* New York: Seabury.

Lieberman, M. L. (1996). *Doors close, doors open: Widows, grieving and growing.* New York: Putnam.

Lifton, R. J. (1993). *The protean self: Human resilience in an age of fragmentation.* New York: Basic Books.

Mahoney, M. J. (1991). *Human change processes.* New York: Basic Books.

Mahrer, A. R. (1996). Existential-humanistic psychotherapy and the religious person. In E. P. Shafranske, (Ed.), *Religion and the clinical practice of psychology* (pp. 433–460). Washington, DC: American Psychological Association.

Malinovsky-Rummell, R., & Hansen, D. J. (1993. Long-term consequences of childhood physical abuse. *Psychological Bulletin, 114*, 68–79.

Martin, L. L., & Tesser, A. (1996). Clarifying our thoughts. In R. S. Wyer (Ed.), *Ruminative thought: Advances in social cognition*, (Vol. 9, pp. 189–209). Mahwah, NJ: Lawrence Erlbaum Associates.

Masterpasqua, F., & Perna, P. A. (1997). *The psychological meaning of chaos: Translating theory into practice.* Washington, DC: American Psychological Association.

McAdams, D. P. (1993). *The stories we live by: Personal myths and the making of the self.* New York: Morrow.

McBride, J. L. (1998). *Spiritual crisis: Surviving trauma to the soul.* New York: Haworth.

McCann, I. L., & Pearlman, L. A. (1990). *Psychological trauma and the adult survivor: Theory, therapy, and transformation.* New York: Brunner/Mazel.

McIntosh, D. N., Silver, R. C., & Wortman, C. B. (1993). Religion's role in adjustment to a negative life event: Coping with the loss of a child. *Journal of Personality and Social Psychology, 65,* 812–821.

Meichenbaum, D. (1994). *A clinical handbook/practical therapist manual for assessing and treating adults with post-traumatic stress disorder (PTSD).* Waterloo, Ontario, Canada: Institute Press.

Miller, J. E. (Speaker). (1989). *How do I go on? Redesigning your future after crisis has changed your life.* (Videotape No. W203). Fort Wayne, IN: Envisions Video Productions.

Miller, J. E. (Speaker). (1993). *The transforming potential of your grief: Eight principles for renewed life* (Cassette Recording No. A205). Fort Wayne, IN: Willowgreen.

Miller, J. E. (Speaker). (1994). *What will help me? Twelve things to remember when you have suffered a loss/How can I help: Twelve things to do when someone you know suffers a loss.* Fort Wayne, IN: Willowgreen.

Miller, J. E. (1995). *Winter grief, summer grace: Returning to life after a loved one dies.* Fort Wayne, IN: Willowgreen.

Mio, J. S., & Katz, A. N. (1996). *Metaphor: Implications and applications.* Mahwah, NJ: Lawrence Erlbaum Associates.

Mutrie, N. (1997). The therapeutic effects of exercise on the self. In K. R. Fox (Ed.), *The physical self: From motivation to well-being* (pp. 287–314). Champaign, IL: Human Kinetics.

Naylor, T. H., Willimon, W. H., & Naylor, M. R. (1994). *The search for meaning.* Nashville, TN: Abingdon.

Neeld, E. H. (1990). *Seven choices: Taking the steps to new life after losing someone you love.* New York: Delta.

Neumann, D. A., & Gamble, S. J. (1995). Issues in the professional development of psychotherapists: Countertransference and vicarious traumatization in the new trauma therapist. *Psychotherapy, 32,* 341–347.

Nolen-Hoeksema, S., McBride, A. & Larson, J. (1997). Rumination and psychological distress among bereaved partners. *Journal of Personality and Social Psychology, 72,* 855–862.

Norris, F. (1992). Epidemiology of trauma: Frequency and impact of potentially traumatic events on different demographic groups. *Journal of Consulting and Clinical Psychology, 60,* 409–418.

O'Leary, V. E., & Ickovics, J. R. (1995). Resilience and thriving in response to challenge: An opportunity for a paradigm shift in women's health. *Women's Health: Research on Gender, Behavior, and Policy, 1,* 121–142.

Overcash, W. S., Calhoun, L. G., Cann, A., & Tedeschi, R. G. (1996). Coping with crises: An examination of the impact of traumatic events on religious beliefs. *Journal of Genetic Psychology, 157,* 455–464.

Owen, N. R., Calhoun, L. G., & Tedeschi, R. G. (1993, August). *Spiritual beliefs and psychotherapy: The views of practicing clinicians.* Presented at the annual meeting of the American Psychological Association, Toronto, Canada.

Pargament, K. I. (1997). *The psychology of religion and coping*. New York: Guilford.

Park, C. L. (1998). Implication of posttraumatic growth for individuals. In R. G. Tedeschi, C. L. Park, & L. G. Calhoun, (Eds.), *Posttraumatic growth: Positive change in the aftermath of crisis* (pp. 153–177). Mahwah, NJ: Lawrence Erlbaum Associates.

Park, C. L., Cohen, L., & Murch, R. (1996). Assessment and prediction of stress-related growth. *Journal of Personality, 64,* 645–658.

Pearlman, L. A., & MacIan, P. S. (1995). Vicarious traumatization: An empirical study of the effects of trauma work on trauma therapists. *Professional Psychology-Research and Practice, 26,* 558–565.

Pearlman, L. A., & Saakvitne, K. W. (1995). *Trauma and the therapist: Countertransference and vicarious traumatization in psychotherapy with incest survivors*. New York: Norton.

Price, R. (1994). *A whole new life*. New York: Antheneum.

Quarantelli, E. L. (1985). An assessment of conflicting views on mental health: The consequences of traumatic events. In C. R. Figley (Ed.), *Trauma and its wake* (Vol. 1, pp. 173–218). New York: Brunner/Mazel.

Raphael, B. (1986). *When disaster strikes*. New York: Basic Books.

Reik, T. (1948). *Listening with the third ear*. New York: Farrar, Straus.

Resnick, H. S., Kilpatrick, D. G., Dansky, B. S., Saunders, B. E., & Best, C. L. (1993). Prevalence of civilian trauma and posttraumatic stress disorder in a representative national sample of women. *Journal of Consulting and Clinical Psychology, 61,* 984–991.

Richards, P. S., & Bergin, A. E. (1997). *A spiritual strategy for counseling and psychotherapy*. Washington, DC: American Psychological Association.

Rogers, C. R. (1961). *On becoming a person*. Boston: Houghton Mifflin.

Rotter, J. B., Chance, J. E., & Phares, E. J. (1972). *Applications of social learning theory of personality*. New York: Holt, Rinehart & Winston.

Rubonis, A. V., & Bickman, L. (1991). Psychological impairment in the wake of disaster: The disaster-psychopathology relationship. *Psychological Bulletin, 109,* 384–399.

Saakvitne, K. W. (1997, November). The rewards of trauma therapy for the therapist. In R. G. Tedeschi (Chair), *Posttraumatic growth in survivors, therapists, researchers, and communities*. Presented at the meeting of the International Society for Traumatic Stress Studies, Montreal, Quebec, Canada.

Schauben, L. J., & Frazier, P. A. (1995). Vicarious trauma: The effects on female counselors working with sexual violence survivors. *Psychology of Women Quarterly, 19,* 49–64.

Schmookler, A. B. (1997). *Living posthumously*. New York: Holt.

Schreurs, K. M., & de Ridder, D. T. (1997). Integration of coping and social support perspectives: Implications for the study of adaptation to chronic diseases. *Clinical Psychology Review 17,* 89–112.

Seligman, M. E. P. (1990). *Learned optimism*. New York: Alfred A. Knopf, Inc.

Selye, H. (1950). *The physiology and pathology of exposure to stress*. Montreal: Acta.

Shafranske, E. P. (1996). Religious beliefs, affiliations, and practices of clinical psychologists. In E. P. Shafranske (Ed.), *Religion and the clinical practice of psychology* (pp. 149–162). Washington, DC: American Psychological Association.

Shay, J. (1994). *Achilles in Vietnam: Combat trauma and the undoing of character.* New York: Antheneum.

Showers, C. J., & Ryff, C. D. (1996). Self-differentiation and well-being in a life transition. *Personality and Social Psychology Bulletin, 22,* 448–460.

Siebert, A. (1996). *The survivor personality.* New York: Perigee Books.

Siegelman, E. Y. (1993). *Metaphor and meaning in psychotherapy.* New York: Guilford.

Strickland, B. R. (1989). Internal-external control expectancies: From contingency to creativity. *American Psychologist, 44,* 1–12.

Taylor, S. E. (1989). *Positive illusions.* New York: Basic Books.

Taylor, S. E., & Brown, J. D. (1988). Illusion and well-being: A social psychological perspective on mental health. *Psychological Bulletin, 103,* 193–210.

Taylor, S. E., & Brown, J. D. (1994). Positive illusions and well-being revisited: Separating fact from fiction. *Psychological Bulletin, 116,* 21–27.

Taylor, S. E., Wayment, H. A., & Collins, M. A. (1993). Positive illusions and affect regulation. In D. M. Wegner & J. W. Pennebaker (Eds.), *Handbook of mental control* (pp. 325–434). Englewood Cliffs, NJ: Prentice-Hall.

Tedeschi, R. G. (1999). Violence transformed: Posttraumatic growth in survivors and their societies. *Aggression and Violent Behavior: A Review Journal, 4,* 319–341.

Tedeschi, R. G., & Calhoun, L. G. (1995). *Trauma and transformation: Growing in the aftermath of suffering.* Thousand Oaks, CA: Sage.

Tedeschi, R. G., & Calhoun, L. G. (1996). The posttraumatic growth inventory: measuring the positive legacy of trauma. *Journal of Traumatic Stress, 9,* 455–471.

Tedeschi, R. G., Park, C. L., & Calhoun, L. G. (Eds.). (1998) *Posttraumatic growth: Positive change in the aftermath of crisis.* Mahwah, NJ: Lawrence Erlbaum Associates.

Tennen, H., & Affleck, G. (1990). Blaming others for threatening events. *Psychological Bulletin, 108,* 209–232.

Tennen, H., & Affleck, G. (1998). Personality and transformation in the face of adversity. In R. G. Tedeschi, C. L. Park, & L., G. Calhoun (Eds.), *Posttraumatic growth: Positive change in the aftermath of crisis* (pp. 65–98). Mahwah, NJ: Lawrence Erlbaum Associates.

Thompson, J., Chung, M. C., & Rosser, R. (1994). The Marchioness disaster: Preliminary report on psychological effects. *British Journal of Clinical Psychology, 33,* 75–77.

Veninga, R. L. (1985). *A gift of hope: How we survive our tragedies.* Boston: Little, Brown.

Veronen, L. J., & Kilpatrick, D. G. (9183). Rape: A precursor to change. In E. J. Callahan & K. A. McCluskey (Eds.), *Life span developmental psychology: Non-normative events* (pp. 167–191). San Diego, CA: Academic Press.

Vrana, S., & Lauterbach, D. (1994). Prevalence of traumatic events and posttraumatic psychological symptoms in a nonclinical sample of college students. *Journal of Traumatic Stress, 7,* 289–302.

Wagner, K. G., & Calhoun, L. G. (1991). Perceptions of social support by suicide survivors and their social networks. *Omega, 23,* 61–73.

Ward, T. B., Smith, S. M., & Vaid, J. (Eds.). (1997). *Creative thought: An investigation of conceptual structures and processes.* Washington, DC: American Psychological Association.

Watzlawick, P., Weakland, J. H., & Fisch, R. (1974). *Change: Principles of problem formation and problem resolution.* New York: Norton.

Weaver, T. L., & Clum, G. A. (1995). Psychological distress associated with interpersonal violence: A meta-analysis. *Clinical Psychology Review, 15,* 115–140.

Weinberg, N., & Williams, J. (1978). How the physically disabled perceive their disabilities. *Journal of Rehabilitation, 44,* 31–33.

Weiss, R., & Parkes, C. M. (1983). *Recovery from bereavement.* New York: Basic Books.

Wills, T. A. (1987). Downward comparison as a coping mechanism. In C. R. Snyder & C. E. Ford (Eds.), *Coping with negative life events: Clinical and social psychological perspectives* (pp. 243–268). New York: Plenum.

Wolin, S. J., & Wolin, S. (1993). *The resilient self: How survivors of troubled families rise above adversity.* New York: Villard.

Wortman, C. B., & Silver, R. C. (1989). The myths of coping with loss. *Journal of Consulting and Clinical Psychology, 57,* 349–357.

Wright, B. A. (1989). Extension of Heider's ideas to rehabilitation psychology. *American Psychologist, 44,* 525–528.

Wuthnow, R. (1991). *Acts of compassion: Caring for others and helping ourselves.* Princeton, NJ: Princeton University Press.

Wuthnow, R. (1994). *Sharing the journey: Support groups and America's new quest for community.* New York: The Free Press.

Yalom, I. (1980). *Existential therapy.* New York: Basic Books.

Yalom, I. (1985). *The theory and practice of group psychotherapy* (3rd ed.). New York: Basic Books.

Yalom, I. D., & Lieberman, M. A. (1991). Bereavement and heightened existential awareness. *Psychiatry, 54,* 334–345.

Yassen, J. (1995). Preventing secondary stress disorder. In C. S. Figley (Ed.), *Compassion fatigue* (pp. 178–208). New York: Brunner/Mazel.

Author Index

Subject Index